WOUNDED AND ON THE RUN

How the worst pain can lead you into your greatest calling

Wendy Parker

D.o.L.L.
MINISTRIES

Daughters of Love & Light
www.dollministries.com
Adelaide, South Australia
info@dollministries.com

© Wendy Parker 2022

ISBN: 9780645508628

All rights reserved. Except for private study, research, criticism or reviews, as permitted under the Copyright Act, no part of this book may be reproduced, stored in a retrieval system, or transmitted in any form or by any means without prior written permission. Enquiries should be made to the publisher.

Publisher's Note: This is a work of non-fiction. Names of persons have been used with permission.

Cataloguing-in-Publications entry is available from the National Library of Australia http:/catalogue.nla.gov.au

Quotes from the Bible are referenced at the conclusion of each chapter.
Referenced scripture taken from the New King James Version®. Copyright © 1982 by Thomas Nelson. Used by permission. All rights reserved.
Referenced scripture taken from The Voice™. Copyright © 2012 by Ecclesia Bible Society. Used by permission. All rights reserved.
Referenced scriptures taken from the Holy Bible, New International Version®, NIV®. Copyright © 1973, 1978, 1984, 2011 by Biblica, Inc.™ Used by permission of Zondervan. All rights reserved worldwide. www.zondervan.com The "NIV" and "New International Version" are trademarks registered in the United States Patent and Trademark Office by Biblica, Inc.™
Referenced scripture taken from the Amplified Bible, Copyright © 2015 by The Lockman Foundation. Used by permission.
Referenced scripture quotations are from The Passion Translation®. Copyright © 2017, 2018, 2020 by Passion & Fire Ministries, Inc. Used by permission. All rights reserved. ThePassionTranslation.com.

Cover and author photo by Lauren Parker

First edition published 2022

'Wendy's powerful story of grace and fire shares how God can use our brokenness to make something beautiful that points to hope, healing and redemption. Readers will be challenged to trust God more fully as we see pain turn into peace.'

Carolyn Miller, bestselling Australian author of historical Christian fiction

'Speaking as an overcomer, Wendy Parker shares raw and vulnerable moments, illuminating the trappings of life and leadership with profound insight. Her practical application offers a hope that we, the reader, may too be healed and whole. How refreshing that this topic would be delivered with such humility, sparing us of any bitter edge, instead bringing the God perspective to the reader in a way that's applicable. With help from 'Wounded and On The Run' you will feel lovingly steered by a dear friend to let go of the past and to step out into brighter days full of calling, promise and potential. These words and this author are the real deal!'

Nathan and Jessica McLean, Hillsong Wollongong Campus Pastors

'Drawing on insights gained in her own valley of trauma and pain, along with lessons learnt whilst faithfully studying the plight of the North American Elk and scripture, Wendy powerfully illustrates how hurt, and disappointment in Church life can lead to a pathway of understanding, healing, and greater intimacy with God — and how we as Christians can protect ourselves from an enemy whose modus operandi is 'shoot to kill.' Wounded And on The Run is a God drop. It's a book in season for the Body of Christ today and a stunning testament to a God who, despite human failings, can heal and restore.'

Nicole Partridge, journalist and writer

'I didn't know how much I needed a book like Wounded & On the Run. The similarities between the elk's journey and the human condition are astonishing, and I found myself immersed in this allegory as I considered my own journey of faith.

My wounds from the hunter - Satan - seemed to have been from another lifetime and, mostly, healed over. But as I journeyed into that cabin in the woods and rested in the presence of God, I felt His Spirit move. He spoke to me through the truths in this book, truths He had told me in His Word but that I hadn't completely accepted. "There is now no condemnation..." He had written. And yet, why was I carrying shame and guilt? I may have stopped bleeding. I may have stopped running. But my scars were barely healed over and could break open at any moment, leaving me vulnerable to the hunter all over again.

On the pages of this book, I not only found a kindred sojourner whose Spirit-filled words led me to the healing balm I so desperately needed, but it also empowered me to regard my scars in a different way. After all, the testimony of Jesus Christ and His immeasurable grace and love is written in these scars of mine. They are the marks of His victory over Satan, sin and death. They are reminders that no matter how deep, wide, or long they are, that nothing can separate me from the love of God. They are the battle scars telling the story of how Jesus rescued and redeemed me, for my good and for His glory.

The truths of this book are so universal. If you've ever been hurt by others - or even yourself - then wander on in to this cabin in the woods. A place of beauty and warmth. A place to rest and reflect. A place saturated with the Spirit of the Almighty God, our loving Father. A place to heal and prepare for the journey ahead.'

Elizabeth Chapman, founder of DOLL Ministries
and author of *Hope Rises: Honest Stories to Honour our Babies in Heaven and Bring Healing to Those Left Behind*

For the Prodigals

Your pain has not been for nothing

'And they overcame him by the blood of the Lamb
and by the word of their testimony'
Revelation 12:11 (NKJV)

A LETTER TO THE READER

I ran for more than 30 years! Not the kind of running that required me to wear athletic training gear and high-tech joggers. I'm talking about internal running—the kind of running you do when you let fear control you. I believe we have all run away from something at some point in our lives—whether it's ourselves, family, friends, commitments, the church, other Christians, God or maybe a calling He has for our life. And while I'm not a trained counsellor, I do know all about internal running. Over three decades I became very acquainted with the art of escaping, until I finally gained enough courage and strength to stop running and let God heal and dress my wounds.

I covered a lot of terrain during those 30 years, going from the highest mountain peaks, down to the deepest, darkest valleys. It wasn't the constant running that finally made me stop and surrender. I could have run much further if it wasn't for the fact that I was bleeding out, leaving a blood trail of brokenness for the hunter, Satan, to line up his scope again and again, and load his weapon of choice, ready to take another shot at me.

Some of the shots the enemy fired came close to being fatal but the hunter knows there's no thrill of the chase if he takes you out of the game completely. He desires to chase the trail of blood you're leaving behind so he can track you down. Better to have you wounded and on the run, making the hunt more exciting and thrilling as he draws ever closer to what he's wanted all along—to finish you off and mount your head upon his already heavily decorated trophy wall.

Did you know that hunters use what is called blood trailing so they can track a wounded elk? The hunter can also tell where the animal has been struck by the colour of the blood left behind. Throughout my story you will find reference to the elk. The unique strength of this majestic animal is what inspired me to write about my wounded past and share with you how God can redeem and restore the inheritance the hunter has stolen from you.

I believe you've picked up this book because you know you are wounded and on the run, and just need a friend who understands your pain. A friend who has let Jesus dress and heal her own wounds and will listen to your story and say, 'Yeah, me too.' I believe it was also placed in your hands for a divine purpose because you are powerful—more powerful than you know—and this is the reason you've been wounded so terribly by the hunter.

From my story of running for so many years, God wanted me to build something for you, dear friend. Something that you could easily find as you searched for a clearing and the way through your forest of pain. And if there's one thing I've learned about God over the years it's that He is faithful. No matter how long you've run or how wounded you are, He will find you.

So, come with me if you will, and picture a scene of a little wooden cabin in the forest with smoke smouldering out of a metal chimney poking through a grey slatted roof. Imagine the dappled rays of light peeking through the branches of the trees, as they shine their warmth on each petal of the colourful flowers adorning the window boxes neatly positioned either side of the front door. Take off your muddied shoes and make yourself at home as you pass under the sign above the door frame, that simply says, 'Welcome' and find a cosy chair in which to rest your weary soul. I've created a safe place for you to sit awhile, where there is no judgement or fault-finding, just a comforting glow from a log fire that offers you its warmth.

This shelter has been tenderly crafted for a wounded soul who is tired from the chase. It is my hope and prayer you will find rest within these pages, and that this is a place for you to catch your breath. Stop running, let Jesus touch your heart and work on your wounds from the inside out. This book will show you how.

INTRODUCTION

The story of my decades of wounding came from inside the church rather than outside of it. Yes, the hunter of your soul isn't scared of using church folk to wound you in your most vulnerable places—this is perhaps one of Satan's worst crimes. But this is not a book about shaming Christians into a confession of their guilt, and casting more shadows over a subject that can often be ignored by the church. The purpose of sharing my story is to shine light where there has been only darkness.

In Isaiah 58:9-12 (NKJV) it promises, '… If you take away the yoke from your midst, The pointing of the finger, and speaking wickedness, If you extend your soul to the hungry And satisfy the afflicted soul, Then your light shall dawn in the darkness, And your darkness shall be as the noonday. The LORD will guide you continually, And satisfy your soul in drought And strengthen your bones; You shall be like a watered garden, And like a spring of water, whose waters do not fail. Those from among you Shall build the old waste places; You shall raise up the foundations of many generations; And you shall be called the Repairer of the Breach, the Restorer of Streets to Dwell In.'

I'm extending my soul to yours, dear friend, because I believe that we are called to build and not tear down. To raise foundations, not to destroy them. This book is a sacred place for your wounds to turn into scars. Because scars are good. They're a way of knowing that what a person is saying is true. It shows someone else you've been through something and come out the other side.

In John 20:25 (NKJV) Thomas says to Jesus, '...Unless I see in His hands the print of the nails, and put my finger into the print of the nails, and put my hand into His side, I will not believe.' Jesus had risen from the tomb and His body was fully restored. So, why would there be any scars? Jesus understood that it was better to show your scars rather than to hide them, so He showed Thomas his scars. However, He went one step further and told Thomas to reach his finger in so he could feel them. Thomas wanted to see Jesus' scars before he believed what the other disciples said was true, but Jesus wanted Thomas to reach in and feel the scars that told the story of what he'd been through. '... Reach your finger here, and look at My hands; and reach your hand *here*, and put *it* into My side' (John 20:27 NKJV). Jesus was not ashamed to show His scars and we shouldn't be either. Like Thomas, I want you to reach into these pages and *feel* Jesus' scars, because it is His scars that will bring your healing, not mine. 1 Peter 2:24 (NIV) reminds us, '... by His wounds you have been healed.'

When my daughter was small, she wouldn't show me her wounds. She'd cover up the cut or graze with her hand and tell me that I was not to look at it. I would tell her that I needed to look at the wound if she wanted me to help her. Reluctantly, after a lot of negotiating and maybe a promise of some ice cream, she would finally reveal her wound so I could clean it up and dress it.

Now she's an adult, I asked her why she would never let me look at her cuts or grazes. She said it was because she was so frightened by my reaction. I have to admit, I could be a little over-dramatic whenever my kids hurt themselves. Like my daughter, we too can hide the wounds we've experienced, but all God wants to do is to help us.

Whether it's the shame or guilt of something we did or something that was done to us, we run and hide because we are scared of God's reaction when we reveal our wounds to Him.

Hiding our wounds and running away has happened since the Garden of Eden. In Genesis 3:9-10 (NKJV), God calls out to Adam and asks where he is. Adam replies, '... I heard Your voice in the garden, and I was afraid because I was naked; and I hid myself.' Adam and Eve suddenly became aware of their nakedness after their encounter with the serpent and were scared of God's reaction, so they hid among the trees.

Listen, dear friend, whether it was something you did or something someone did to you, God isn't going to overreact. He wants to take a look at your wounds so He can help you. I think we forget that Jesus was wounded long before we felt the sting of rejection, betrayal, or disappointment in our lives. In Isaiah 53:4-5 (NKJV) it says, 'Surely He has borne our griefs and carried our sorrows; yet we esteemed Him stricken, smitten by God, and afflicted. But He *was* wounded for our transgressions, He *was* bruised for our iniquities; the chastisement for our peace was upon Him, and by His stripes we are healed.'

Did you catch that? Jesus endured the breaking so we could become whole, and this was done for us through His suffering and humiliation. You think that there is no hope for you, but there is. Jesus leaves the ninety-nine to look for the one. The Father is standing by the gate, scanning the horizon and waiting for the prodigal to return home again. You can't keep running and bleeding out like this—you need to rest and be healed. I know, it sounds a painful process to go through, my friend, but the hunter of your soul isn't far behind and he is already reloading his weapon for the next shot.

PART ONE

WOUNDED AND ON THE RUN

CHAPTER ONE

Rebel Heart

'The one who has no wounds has never fought a battle.'[1]
ERWIN MCMANUS

'A bull elk can easily cover miles of rugged country in that amount of time, especially if he is wounded or on the run.'[2] This sentence from John Eldredge's book, *Wild at Heart*, leapt off the page at me. The book had sat on my bookshelf for many years, and I don't know what led me to pick it up again, but something awakened and stirred within me that day. I started to research the North American elk, and when I found out that it is known as a spirit animal symbolising strength and stamina,[3] I knew I needed to share my story. I don't claim to be an expert on this animal, however, the similarities between the wounded elk and a wounded Christian are fascinating.

The elk is also game that is hunted. Known as blood trailing, the hunter goes on a chase to track down the elk after shooting it with a bullet or an arrow. Blood seeping from the elk's wound is left on trees and branches as it runs through the forest, leaving a blood trail which the hunter follows. When the elk cannot run anymore, the patient hunter will line up his scope or pull back his bow and fire the fatal shot or arrow which will end the animal's life.

My blood trail started when I found myself in an abortion clinic two weeks before my 17th birthday. Up until then, I had managed to keep up the appearance of the good Christian church girl. Successfully keeping my secret of under-aged drinking and nightclubbing from my God-fearing parents. The abortion would be just another secret hidden within the depths of my heart. The intention too, was that every feeling for my unborn child would be stuffed deep down in my soul together with all my other disappointments. Ethically, terminating an unwanted pregnancy has many issues surrounding it. However, I believe at the heart of the matter is fear. Fear can lead you to a decision that you would otherwise be against if it were perhaps happening to someone else. But when difficult situations confront you, all your morals and Christian values can fly out the window. I knew the Sixth Commandment in Exodus 20:13 (NIV), 'You shall not murder' but I just couldn't go through with having the baby. My biggest fear was the fact that my parents would find out.

Throughout my childhood, my mum would warn my sister and I, 'You'd better not get pregnant before you get married.' Laying in that hospital bed was exactly where I didn't want to be. My boyfriend at the time (who is now my husband of 27 years) was just as scared as I was. He told me that he would support me whether I kept our baby or not—it was my choice. I agonised over the decision to terminate my pregnancy. I believe on that day, I didn't just abort my baby, I aborted my relationship with God too. I had stopped attending church because I felt completely abandoned by God, and I believe it was from that wound that I also abandoned my child.

You wonder, even though you've run away from church and Christians as far as you possibly can, why doesn't God stop you running? Why is it, '...you have hedged me behind and before...' (Psalm 139:5 NKJV), and yet that doesn't stop us? Wouldn't a hedge protect?

Surely, God wouldn't just let you walk right into the hunter's trap and take a bite from the forbidden fruit! If He is the Alpha and the Omega, the end from the beginning, why does He just stand by and let you go through all the pain and suffering? It's in these moments too, you hear the answers from well-meaning Christians, 'Well, you know, His ways are higher than our own' or the classic response, 'God must be trying to teach you something.' Of course, these and many more answers of why we go through pain and suffering at the hands of the hunter, do not help nor have any theological merit. Suffering from bad choices can make you question God's character, and as I lay in that hospital bed of the abortion clinic, I wanted to know why God had abandoned me.

According to the Collins Dictionary, the word *abandon* means, 'to desert or leave: to give up completely: to give oneself over completely to an emotion.'[4] I had given up completely on having a relationship with God, and decided that I had been wounded beyond saving now.

Besides, why would God want me back now that I'd done something so terrible?

It has been over 30 years since I made that decision to terminate my pregnancy, and there are moments when it feels like it happened just yesterday. Decisions like this can have a long-lasting effect, well after the physical pain of the operation has gone. At the time, I wouldn't allow myself to grieve the loss. I had shut the door on my heart and thrown away the key. And as I left the abortion clinic that day, my false belief of abandonment from God was the golden shot the hunter so desperately needed to start the blood trail.

Hunters go to a lot of effort to track a wounded elk. After spending the whole weekend blood trailing an elk over rough, mountainous terrain, most hunters leave empty-handed having nothing to show for their efforts. However, Satan does not give up that easily. He is a very patient and savvy hunter, and his up-front preparation requires the careful process of observing you first. Looking back over my childhood and teenage years, I now realise that experiences in my home and church life represented shot after shot of rejection, guilt and shame orchestrated by the hunter to take me out and to stop me loving Jesus. Matthew 18:3 beckons us to become like little children so we can enter the kingdom of heaven, and my love for Jesus had always been childlike to the core. Clearly, this beautiful relationship was a threat to the hunter as he tried time and again to wound me and wear me down.

Maybe like me, you've had to make a difficult and life-changing decision or had a poor start in life which has led you down a path away from God. Or maybe it was Christians whose choices made you question if God was real. Perhaps you feel too damaged and too broken, thinking that your wounds somehow disqualify you from having any kind of relationship with God. Don't believe the lie from Satan that Jesus will reject you. He longs to draw near to you.

Psalm 103:3 (TPT), is a comfort to our wounded souls and says, 'You kissed my heart with forgiveness in spite of all I've done …' God longs to have intimacy with you. When Satan was shut out of heaven because pride filled his heart, he lost intimacy with God, and he knows that when you discover intimacy with God, you're powerful.

A skilful hunter knows that it's not how the hunt starts but how it finishes. So too with God—how you start in life isn't as important to Him as how you will finish. Despite my choices, God, in His kindness blessed my husband, Philip and I with a son some years later after we were married. We named him Samuel which means, 'Told by God'. Even though Philip wasn't a Christian and I had run away from the church, I believe God had His loving hand on us as we decided on a name for our baby boy. Four years later we were blessed again by God and I gave birth to a daughter. We named her, Lauren which is derived from the name, Laura meaning, 'a crown made from the leaves of the bay laurel which was given to heroes or victors.' Blessed with a boy and a girl, I truly felt, and still feel like a victor.

Now that our children have grown into fine adults, I see them show compassion and empathy toward young girls who have found themselves in the same situation as their mother did all those years ago. But above all else, it is the compassion and empathy they show toward me.

They tell me that they don't blame me for what I did, they just admit a touch of sadness that they weren't able to meet their older brother or sister here on earth. As a family, we look forward to the day when we will all meet our lost family member, face to face in heaven.

Revelation 21:4 (NKJV) promises that, '…God will wipe away every tear from their eyes; there shall be no more death, nor sorrow, nor crying. There shall be no more pain, for the former things have passed away.' Even though you know there is forgiveness, and by God's wonderful grace and mercy He has cast the wrong choices we have made into the depths of the sea (Micah 7:19 paraphrased), there is still a part of you, deep within your soul that wishes the clock could be turned back to that moment, right before making a decision that changed the trajectory of your life. However, you can only move forward. Psalm 139:4-5 (TPT) says, '… You know every step I will take before my journey even begins. You've gone into my future to prepare the way, and in kindness, you follow behind me to spare me from the harm of my past.'

So, if God goes into our future and prepares the way, why does He follow behind instead of stopping us make the wrong choices? It's because He gives us free will. Again, consider Adam and Eve. Why didn't God ride into the garden on his noble steed and rescue them from making a decision they would regret for the rest of their lives? You see, God doesn't want us to be mindless robots who cannot think for ourselves. Free will is His gift to us. We get to choose whether we will follow His ways or make our own choices. Psalm 139:24 (TPT) helps us to choose a better path, one that will lead back to God—'See if there is any path of pain I'm walking on, and lead me back to your glorious, everlasting ways—the path that brings me back to you.'

I pray that my story will show you compassion and bring understanding, and I encourage you to invite Jesus into the pain of your past. He is the only one who can heal the wounds that were inflicted on you, and to correct the false belief that some of your wounding you have inflicted upon yourself. The hunter will only ever lead you down the wrong path to keep you running from God's promises. However, God is never far behind, gently leading you back to the right path of His glorious and everlasting ways. You just need to let Him heal your wounds until all you are left with are victorious scars.

Endnotes: Chapter One

Ref 1   McManus Raphael Erwin. *The Way Of The Warrior: An Ancient Path To Inner Peace,* WaterBrook, an imprint of the Crown Publishing Group, a division of Penguin Random House LLC, New York: 2019. Page 196

Ref 2   Eldredge John. *Wild at Heart*, Nashville, Tennessee, Thomas Nelson: 2001. Page 2.

Ref 3   https://dreamingandsleeping.com/elk-spirit-animal-symbolism-and-meaning/

[4]*Collins Paperback Dictionary.* Bishopbriggs, Glasgow, HarperCollins Publishers: 1999.

CHAPTER TWO

Sifted like Wheat

'My whole life I've had the fear that I was going to be abandoned.'
HALLE BERRY

I said the salvation prayer when I was seven years old. My mum had been taking my older sister and I to church for a while and I remember sitting on the kitchen bench top, chatting with her as she prepared dinner one afternoon. I don't know what I said for mum to ask me if I wanted Jesus to live in my heart, but I knew that I quite liked this Jesus we had sung about in the weekly school assemblies. I would sing songs to Jesus as I swung my legs back and forth on my swing in our garden, going higher and higher until I felt I could touch the sky. Those long summer northern hemisphere nights that saw the sun stay up way past my bedtime, I found myself lost in the solace and peace of singing the same song over and over again to Jesus. I wondered if I invited Jesus to live inside of my heart, He could be the friend who would be able to fix the chaos inside our home which would fix the chaos inside of me.

    Throughout my early childhood years growing up in England, I don't remember a day went by where I didn't live in fear of mum acting on her constant threats to leave dad. That feeling of abandonment made me not want to go to school at times in case mum decided to leave and never come back while I was at school, and this thought petrified me.

    When mum worked her evening shifts at the pub, dad looked after us. One evening while we were laughing and doing our usual play fight routine, where dad faked surrender because my sister and I were so 'strong', he thought it would be funny to throw a black, rubber spider he had purchased at myself and my sister. I screamed and then cried. After that, I wanted to go with mum everywhere, to the point where I would sit at the bottom of the stairs with my coat and shoes on while she was getting ready for work. Each time mum tried to leave for work, I would cling onto her tighter, sobbing, and dad would have to pull me off her. The spider prank continued, until one day mum found out why I didn't want her to leave for work.

    I remember mum arguing with dad about the rubber spider that I loathed, and he promised he would get rid of it. I believed him. However, a few weeks later he threw the spider at me again, and when I told mum she became so angry that she grabbed a box of matches and the rubber spider in one hand and my hand in her other hand and marched out the back door, past the rockery, past my swing, past the veggie patch, to a small slab of concrete in the garden. I can remember it all so clearly as she lit the match that ignited the rubber spider into flames. My sister came to join us for our 'spider burning ceremony', and as I watched its red eyes burn and its yellow spots that covered its back slowly melt into a blob on the concrete, I felt relieved. It was gone forever. However, the constant arguing, and fighting continued as dad drunk away the mortgage money and we'd find him occasionally, passed out on the bathroom floor from the alcohol he'd consumed. All this chaos developed deep, emotional wounds in me which resulted in bedwetting most nights.

Thankfully, things improved dramatically in our family when mum finally talked dad into coming along to a prayer meeting one evening at our church and he had a supernatural experience with Jesus. Everything changed. But throughout those turbulent years growing up, one thing that never changed was my bedwetting habit. Mum believed the doctor when he said, *'she'll grow out of it'* which resulted in my parents doing nothing about it.

It wasn't until I turned nineteen that mum thrust a leaflet at me and told me to do something about my problem. The leaflet had a phone number of a doctor who specialised in incontinence issues, and within a few months of counselling, I was dry every night. No more hiding. No more camouflaging my wet patches on my clothes. No more soaked, wrecked mattresses. For the first time in my life, I felt heard and understood. I cannot remember the doctor's name, but I am forever grateful to him.

The Shawnee Indian's call the elk, Wapiti, which means 'white rump',[1] referring to the animal's unique wheat-coloured coat. In the North American elk's natural habitat of forests, alpine meadows, prairies, and uninhabited valleys [2] they graze on grasses and the colouring of their coats help to keep them hidden from any predators. An elk never wants to bring attention to itself, and its wheat-coloured coat keeps it blended into its surroundings.

Experienced hunters study the behavioural patterns of an elk so they can lure it towards the place where they can get the clear shot they need. Unless the elk moves into an open space, the hunter will lose sight of the animal quickly because its coat helps camouflage it into the background.

As I think about the wheat-coloured coat of the elk, I wonder if in that moment when I said 'yes' to Jesus while sitting on the kitchen bench top, deciding to switch my allegiance from the dark shadows of the enemy's kingdom and move into the light, open space of God's kingdom, my wheat-coloured coat that once kept me hidden, the plain brown wrapper which blended me into this world, the cloak of my culture which concealed my whereabouts could no longer keep me hidden from the hunter. At seven years old in the humble surroundings of our kitchen, my wheat-coloured camouflage was yielded, and the royal colours of my true identity were revealed, communicating to the hunter, Satan, that my gutsy move had declared me a defector.

Where are you right now dear friend? Hiding in the shadows of the dark forest, afraid to act on the whisper you hear in the wind that calls you by name? Or are you the brave elk that has decided to say 'yes' to Jesus, but now you feel exposed because the camouflage of your wheat-coloured coat has been shed and the royal colours of your true identity are revealed, initiating the hunter's arrow which will start a blood trail?

I know. I understand that it's not easy to come out from the safety and remoteness of the dense forest and stand in the open space of your beliefs. Growing up in a dysfunctional home which left me to deal with the emotional, internal struggles of camouflaging my bedwetting right throughout my childhood up until I was nineteen years old, can pick at the scars that evaluate your loyalty to God's kingdom and wonder if it's all worth it. Even now, the sense of abandonment sometimes leaves its shadow across my heart when I feel discarded and devalued by people that I love.

Forsaken. The word sounds so weighty, so final. And each time I read Jesus' words he cried out from the cross, *'Eli, Eli, lama sabachthani?'* [3] the scars within me sting as I remember the pain found in the burn of feeling abandoned. Our lament echoes the emotions of Jesus as we too cry out in a loud voice, *'My God, My God, why have you forsaken Me?'* until our throats are hoarse from the questions, we ask Him.

Why have You...?

Why have You left me to run in the wrong direction?

Why have You let the hunter pierce my soul with his arrows?

Why have You let the stream of blood flow out from my wounds that keep the hunter tracking me down time and time again?

Why God?

Sifting Season

In Luke 22: 31-32 Jesus foresees Peter's denial. 'Peter, my dear friend, listen to what I'm about to tell you. Satan has obtained permission to come and sift you all like wheat and test your faith. But I have prayed for you, Peter, that you would stay faithful to me no matter what comes. Remember this: after you have turned back to me and have been restored, make it your life mission to strengthen the faith of your brothers.'[4] Jesus knows when you step out into the clearing of the forest, you're vulnerable to the hunter's assault that's why he tells Peter that he has prayed for him before the first arrow from the hunter's bow penetrates his fleshy nature. Note that the verse states that Satan has obtained permission.

Who did Satan go to for permission to sift us all like wheat? For that answer we need to look at Job 1:6-12.

'Now there was a day when the sons of God came to present themselves before the Lord, and Satan also came among them. And the Lord said to Satan, 'From where do you come?' So, Satan answered the Lord and said, 'From going to and fro on the earth, and from walking back and forth on it.' Then the Lord said to Satan, 'Have you considered My servant Job, that there is none like him on the earth, a blameless and upright man, one who fears God and shuns evil? So, Satan answered the Lord and said, 'Does Job fear God for nothing? Have You not made a hedge around him, around his household, and around all that he has on every side? You have blessed the work of his hands, and his possessions have increased in the land. But now, stretch out Your hand and touch all that he has, and he will surely curse You to Your face!' And the Lord said to Satan. 'Behold, all that he has is in your power; only do not lay a hand on this person.' So, Satan went out from the presence of the Lord.'[5]

It's hard to comprehend that a God who claims He is love allows Satan to sift you like wheat. The concept around this passage resembles the process of sifting wheat. The point of sifting is to separate the genuine wheat from other things that are mixed in with it.[6] Jesus knew Peter would deny Him out of his fear and uncertainty of what the future held. Therefore Jesus specifically prayed for Peter so after the sifting from Satan, after the testing, Peter would stay faithful, and his faith would be restored.

Fill a Tag

Hunting tags help wildlife management agencies regulate the population of local animals by allowing them to reduce the number of kills per year, preventing over hunting.[7] A tag is a physical documentation the hunter must carry and is filled out by the hunter after the hunt. The tag must be attached to the animal and filled in promptly after the animal has been killed. This is called, 'fill your tag'. A tag means a hunter has the legal authority to kill one individual animal and comes with restrictions as to where a hunter can hunt and what they can hunt.[8] A properly filled out tag has to have the location, month, date, and time of the kill to help conservationists manage the hunting season.

    Sadly, I listen to many believers tell me of their disappointment because their family members or a friend have been subjected to the hunter, Satan, filling out his tag and attaching it to their lost and wounded souls, revealing the location, month, date, and time where he finally managed to kill off their faith. They have believed the lie that their family members or friend are too far gone for restoration because the tag has been filled. They feel that it's over, and there is no hope for their recovery. Too many setbacks have caused their faith to exhale and breathe no more, and so, the hunter, Satan uses this as leverage to trap many believers' thinking into a Good Friday mindset, waving the documentation in their faces reminding them that he has indeed filled in the tag and been given the authority to sift a person's faith as believers prepare spices for a proper burial.

Standing at a Distance

Hard to imagine the disappointment the disciples felt as they watched on with broken hearts as their Saviour, their King, and their friend slowly died an agonising death on a wooden cross. All the miracles they'd seen Him do, every parable He'd explained to them, each promise about His kingdom coming, was for what. This? Perhaps they had set their expectations a little too high? Maybe this final lesson was to show them how hard it was going to be to carry on in their disappointment and unavoidable pain as their emotions consumed them while preparing to bury their friend. As the saying goes, 'time heals all wounds' but not these. Not the deep wounding of setback, failure, disappointment, and defeat. And as the crowd dwindled away on the hill at Calvary, the few disciples that stayed until Jesus took His last breath, stood at a distance. 'The crowds of common people who had gathered and watched the whole ordeal through to its conclusion left for their homes, pounding on their chests in profound grief. And all who know Jesus personally, including the group of women who had been with him from the beginning in Galilee, stood at a distance, watching all of these things unfold.'[9]

The reason why the women stood at a distance was that no one could stand too close to a crucifixion because they would obstruct the macabre view of the spectacle, so family and friends had to stand at a distance so everyone could see the execution clearly. Isn't that true of us also? Whether it was a family member's faith, a friend's, or even own faith that the hunter, Satan managed to fill the tag on, we feel the familiar sting of the wound of disappointment, of things not turning out as we had hoped for and planned, so we decide to stand away from the cross at a distance. We roll the heavy stone over the entrance of the tomb where dead faith lies because we've read the tag the hunter has filled in. The tag that reminds us of the location, month, date, and time the hunter, Satan obtained permission to come and sift us all like wheat.

Our Good Friday mindset is decidedly deceptive as the falsehood that the redemptive blood that flowed down the beam of the cross is not powerful enough to heal anyone's wrecked and wounded soul. And as we prepare our spices for a proper burial of our faith or someone else's, we search through our memories and find others whom we have long forgotten because we've read the tag the hunter attached to the carcass of their faith. The dear family members or friends that once knew Jesus personally, who'd been with Him from the beginning but decided to roll the stone over their faith on Good Friday, believing that the tag dangling around the foot of their faith means that there will be no resurrection Sunday for them. Disappointed disciples standing at a distance, mourning over the remains of their faith, reading the filled out tag with all the gruesome details of a successful blood trail and hunt.

The Borrowed Space

I was a disappointed disciple who stood at a safe distance from the cross for many years. At least I thought it was safe, until I discovered that the distance between myself and the cross was never safe because it just left more room for the hunter, Satan to fire his arrows at me, leaving my wounds of disappointment to bleed out until he filled in his tag and tied it to the foot of my dead faith. However, the great news about a Good Friday mentality is its only part of the story because no matter how dead a faith looks in the natural, resurrection Sunday is coming. However, for Sunday to come, we need to stop running. 'Early on Sunday morning, even before the sun had fully risen, these two women made their way back to the tomb with the spices and ointments they had prepared. When they arrived, they found the stone was rolled away from the tomb entrance, and when they looked inside, the body of the Lord Jesus was nowhere to be seen...As they stood there in confusion, two men suddenly appeared standing beside them. These men seemed to glow with light. The women were so terrified that they fell to the ground facedown. 'Why are you seeking the living One in the place of the dead? He is not here. He has risen from the dead.'[10]

The tomb was just a space Jesus borrowed on Good Friday before His powerful resurrection on Sunday morning. We need to correct the old saying that 'time heals all wounds' because time cannot heal all our setbacks, failures, and disappointments which have caused deep wounding. Only the resurrecting blood of Jesus heals *ALL* wounds. The hunter, Satan may have sifted your faith or someone else's faith with every arrow of disappointment and grief. Now you're looking at the tag he's gladly filled in, the one the hunter has tied to the foot of faith, letting you believe the lie that there's just no hope of a resurrection. The faith is dead, buried, and departed. The tomb is sealed, so what's the point? But let me encourage you dear friend, no matter how lifeless, cold, and stiff someone's faith may seem, if we stop standing at a distance and choose to move toward the beam where the remnant of Jesus' precious blood has stained the wood, lean in and take a closer look, we'll find a filled in tag tied to the foot of cross. A tag with these words written on it, 'You are not abandoned.'

Endnotes: Chapter Two

Ref 1   visitestespark.com/blog post/8 Fascinating facts about Elk. By Tyler Wilcox on May 6th 2019

Ref 2   Elk – Description, habitat, image, diet, and interesting facts. animals.net/elk/

Ref 3   Matthew 27:46. *Spiritual Warfare Bible.* 2012 Lake Mary, Florida, Charisma House

Ref 4   Luke 22:31-32. *The Passion Translation: New Testament with Psalms, Proverbs, and Song of Songs, Second Edition.* Passion & Fire Ministries, Inc. BroadStreet Publishing: 2018.

Ref 5   Job 1:6-12. *Spiritual Warfare Bible.* 2012 Lake Mary, Florida, Charisma House

Ref 6   Keener, Craig S. 1993. *The IVP Bible Background Commentary: New Testament.* Downers Grove, Ill. InterVarsity Press.

Ref 7   modernhunters.com/hunting seasons-and-tags/

Ref 8   mossyoak.com/our-obsession/blogs.

Ref 9   Luke 23:48-49. Ecclesia Bible Society. 2012. *The Voice Bible: Step into the Story of Scripture.* Nashville: Thomas Nelson

Ref 10   Luke 24:1-6. Ecclesia Bible Society. 2012. *The Voice Bible: Step into the Story of Scripture.* Nashville: Thomas Nelson

CHAPTER THREE

The Best Defence is to Run

'When you believe a lie, you empower the liar.'[1]
BILL JOHNSON

Elks communicate by a roaring and whistling sound that moves through their lips and nostrils.[2] These sounds are known as bugle calls. Bugling is especially used during the mating season and young bull elks will use a series of bugle calls to round up and secure their cows early in the season. However, when a more developed bull elk arrives and decides to pick a fight with a younger bull so he can pilfer the young bull's harem, the younger bull will retreat because they know their survival rate is low if they choose to fight against a mature, contentious bull elk who has impressive points that make up the rack on its head.[3] If a young bull elk is seen running, it could possibly mean that a more mature bull elk has taken his cows. The hunter knows the young elk is now vulnerable because it has left the herd behind which places the elk in a perfect position for the hunter to shoot.

Hunter's use the elk's bugle call to their advantage and can entice an elk to come closer by blowing into a device called a diaphragm. This efficient method of faking an elk's bugle call has been the demise of many young elks, and a well-rehearsed, volume-controlled bugle call can be the bait some bulls find hard to resist if the hunter has done his homework. An experienced hunter puts themselves in the mentality of an elk, so their fake bugle calls have a convincing sound which make the elk believe the call is real.[4]

An elk wounded and on the run is the adventure that gets a hunter's blood pumping. If the set-up of the fake bugle calls have been effective, then the hunter can manage to get a good wound shot for the blood trail to begin. The mock sounds and calls can deceive the judgment of even the savviest of elks because an experienced hunter becomes an expert in making the bugle call sound authentic.

A Convincing Sound

Looking back, my parents probably should never have decided to follow the reverend that impressed everyone with his gifted communication skills at our church one Sunday morning. His charisma and charm slowly encouraged many over the course of a few months to rethink their loyalty and membership to the Assemblies Of God which our family had been an important part of. I remember dad coming home late from work most evenings because he was committing every spare moment to helping the workmen build the new A.O.G. church. The old hut we worshiped in was destined for demolition and after many months of prayer, sacrifice, and contributions to the church building fund my parents had, along with many others we did life with, began to see a miracle being built one brick at a time.

Now, only a few years later, it felt as though the foundations had only just settled in our new church building as our faithful pastor and his wife watched on broken hearted when half the congregation walked out and followed the dynamic reverend because of arguments over rigid mindsets in the leadership that were presumed to have been built along with the new church walls. I was almost fourteen and I didn't really understand all the church politics surrounding this move of my parents. But I do remember listening to discussions at home about the pastor and his wife warning my parents not to leave the established A.O.G. and join the reverend's brand-new church named, 'Faith Fellowship' which was to be held in a community hall over the other side of town.

The transition to the new church helped me to become a part of a tight-knit bunch of teenagers who made up our youth group and I loved the connection we all had. But, like me, they all had baggage from their pasts that hadn't been dealt with, and so I went from a shy, apprehensive, cautious girl who had been dealing with internal issues, to a promiscuous, foolhardy teenager who didn't know how to handle all the attention from boys. For a while church was great, and our youth group was allowed to occasionally perform drama skits of Bible stories in our Sunday evening services. We had a crèche that was ran by an eighteen-year-old woman who had answered an advert our church had put in the local newspaper to look after all the toddlers and babies while the service was going on.

Writing all this I can now see the hunter, Satan, circling me ready for the hunt, deciding which weapon would be the most effective to wound me as he blew his fake bugle calls to bring me in. In my own naïve, reckless teenaged thinking I didn't really go to church for sound teaching, right theology, or to build a strong faith. I went because my friends were there. I felt I still loved Jesus, so I continued to do 'Christian' things even though my ill-advised actions told a different story.

Over time the lady who looked after the crèche and I became friends which meant I spent more time in the crèche than the church service. One Sunday, she asked me if I wanted to go with her to a nightclub the following week. By now I had turned fifteen, so I felt totally ready to take my secret teenaged rebellion to the next level. The combination of being tall, having a nice smile, dressing in the right clothes, and hanging around my eighteen-year-old friend got me into nightclubs surprisingly easy. I don't know how I stayed safe during that season, but I'm sure my mum's prayers and an angel assigned from heaven to protect me had something to do with it.

One evening in church an evangelist came to preach. I was sitting in the back row bored with the whole church thing and wondering why I kept showing up each week, (probably because my parents made me) when the guest preacher suddenly looked at me and said this.

'Wendy, God has his hand on you for a purpose. I believe that God has His hand on you for leadership, but I believe that in God having His hand upon you, tonight, He wants you to make a fresh and new decision to go His way. He's got some exciting things in store for you. God's love is towards you, and you know, you've actually needed that love and it's almost like you've been starved of it for a while and God is saying tonight, He wants to re-establish you in a friendship with Him. He wants

you to hear his heartbeat, He wants you to experience intimacy with Him. He wants you tonight, just to come back into that love. Let that love come again to the place, you see, where no friend, nor nobody else can understand. Nobody else can meet that need either, only God! God is calling you. You know exactly what I'm talking about! Wendy, let's get this thing together, come back and let's move again. You can be used to win many, many thousands of people to Christ, or you can just throw your life away. It's your choice! But He is calling you to friendship and into love tonight. You're a leader, you either lead people away or lead people to Him. It's a big responsibility!'

I am convinced my mum had the spirit of Habakkuk as she often tape-recorded sermons so she could write things down. Like the prophet of old she wrote, '...the vision and engrave it plainly on [clay] tablets so that the one who reads it will run. For the vision is yet for the appointed [future] time it hurries toward the goal [of fulfilment]; it will not fail.'[5] I decided to listen to the call from God and start the journey to remedy my rebellious ways. The evangelist invited me to a YWAM weekend and while there I was filled with the Holy Spirit which was the first step toward making a *'fresh new decision to go His way'*. And even though the words the evangelist had spoken over me felt overwhelming and daunting, I sensed that God had given me a seed of a promise. But in the giving of the promise, God still gave me a choice of whether I would lead people to Him or away from Him. Was it a responsibility I was ready for?

Believing A Lie

A prophesy is used for repentance, for someone to turn around their ways but 'the divine purpose in prophecy is mainly to stimulate a faithful response in the present not to provide an absolute blueprint for an uncertain future.' [6] Satan knows for each prophesy to be fulfilled we must faithfully respond to God's call. We have to listen out for the real bugle call that keeps us running toward the future He has planned for us.

    I knew the prophesy was a genuine call from God because I felt something stir inside of me as the evangelist was speaking the words that evening in church. And yet, in my rebellion, in my misguided advice from my youth group friends, I had grown so accustomed to listening and following the hunter's counterfeit bugle calls that I didn't see him lining up his scope and move closer toward me. The accusation shots the hunter, Satan, fired at me in the church foyer one evening after a service narrowly missed my heart and hit me straight in the lung area. The first shot came when a man who had been hanging around with us in our youth group for a few months became angry because I told him I wasn't interested in his advances and to leave me alone. Not liking the rejection, he grabbed my arm and starting shouting at me which alerted the reverend to come out into the foyer. I thought he would tell my accuser how inappropriate his behaviour was toward me because he was much older than myself, and I was clearly getting upset by what was happening. But instead of helping me the reverend fired more shots, peppering me with a barrage of insults and accusations that were so fierce it caused sweat to run down his forehead and turn his face to a deep shade of crimson. By now mum had come out into the foyer to see what all the commotion was about, and I hoped she would put a stop to the verbal abuse. But despite my tears and pleas, she decided to side with the reverend, letting me know that all this chaos had been brought on by myself. In that moment I felt sure dad would come out to the foyer to help me by saying something, anything to protect his youngest daughter from this assault. However, he said nothing to defend or protect me and his uninvolved attitude of the situation had sealed my fate.

Bang, bang, bang...
And as the pink, frothy blood seeped out from my lung area, the bullets from the hunter's rifle made it hard for me to breathe. I felt the ache of abandonment from my childhood all over again. Doubts circled my thoughts about the prophetic word that had been spoken over me a few months prior from the evangelist. He seemed so kind and gentle, so different from the condemnation I now felt from the reverend's aggressive behaviour. I wondered if I was indeed too impure and carnal minded for the promise to be real, because why would a good God want anything to do with a bad, teenaged girl like me?

I remember the conversation on the walk home was painfully restrained between myself and my parents. I was confused because whenever I chose to tell my parents about someone bullying me at school, dad would take the next day off work and go and see the headmaster first thing in the morning. He'd fight for me, defend my case, causing the bully to retreat. What had happened? Why was I being blamed? I pledged to myself when I reached the safety of my bedroom, that my best defence was to run from the closeness of God, doing life on my own from now on because the people in the church had let me down so badly.

Empowering A Deceiver

Phony bugle calling is the hunter's tactic of taking advantage of something an elk naturally does. If you've decided to follow Jesus, then you'll naturally want to know what His voice sounds like. Listen long enough to real bugle calls and you'll naturally find acceptance, hope and truth from other believers that no fake bugle call could ever promise you.

But confusion sets in when your ears are so used to listening to the hunter's fake calls that you're not sure what a real bugle call sounds like when you hear it. Wounded by the very ones who call themselves 'Christ followers' believing they have been looking out for your well-being is a heavy blow to your confidence. You start to become disorientated and disconnected spiritually when a man of God who has preached love, compassion, and forgiveness at the pulpit each Sunday shouts abuse at you. Distrust follows when a leader who has convinced your parents that his bugle call to start a church was the authentic sound of God. You become confused because you cannot figure out why a reverend, a man of God, would prefer to pull the trigger on the hunter's rifle rather than choose to disarm it.

The tactic of the hunter, Satan, is to drown out the genuine bugle call from God with his lies so that our ears do not become accustomed to the sound of God's voice. Once you recognise God's call on your life your natural response is to respond with repentance. A call that let's God know you want to turn around from the path that's been leading you away from Him and go back to where you felt safe. Communication between God and the believer is the connection needed to bring us back into the safety of the herd and an authentic, genuine call will help locate where you are. When we know His voice and recognise His call, we'll never follow the strange, conflicting sounds of false messiahs and self-appointed leaders again [7] because we can confidently run to the Good Shepherd instead of running away from Him.

An Opportune Moment

Interestingly, elk are the favourite prey of wolves, and an antlerless bull can be an easy target for a hungry wolf.[8] Wolves are shrewd hunters and as they follow a herd of elk, they are weighing up one that is gesturing any form of weakness. Like the hunter, wolves adjust their approach depending on the weather conditions. A snowfall can be especially helpful to a hunter when blood trailing elk as the spots of blood are more visible. Wolves use the winter months to gain advantage in the hunt, knowing that elks are less likely to outrun them in snow. A wolf waits for an opportune moment to execute a successful hit.[9]

Sadly, the impact of the abuse I had somehow justifiably earned in the church foyer that Sunday evening caused my older sister to withdraw from the church too. She realised, like myself, that the charismatic leader my parents had left the A.O.G. church for, was nothing but a sheep rustler in wolf's clothing. Jesus warns us in Matthew 7:15 to beware of the false teachers who's covering appears to look like an innocent sheep, but internally they are ravenous wolves.[10]

Strangely, none of what happened to me in the church foyer seemed to bother my parents. As far as their faulty belief system and strong allegiance to the fellowship were concerned,

I was meant to be the one apologising! I was dumbstruck and couldn't believe what mum was saying. The fact that they believed that I *deserved* the abusive outburst from the reverend because of my immature choices didn't seem fair.

And there it was.

The salty sting of abandonment rubbing into my wounds once again.

Wolf in Sheep's Clothing

The persuasion techniques of the charismatic reverend, managed to convince my parents he hadn't done anything wrong. Clearly, this wolf in sheep's clothing had certainly pulled the wool over my parent's eyes as they seriously believed that a church that started with no board of directors and a *very* loose structure of leadership was an authentic call from God. How did they get so deceived?

About a couple of years later my parents stopped attending Faith Fellowship because of revelations about the reverend's past had emerged. Truths about hidden secrets in the leadership were brought out into the light as the scales finally fell away from my parents' eyes as they shared bizarre stories of the reverend's threatening tactics. They told me that he once warned the congregation, that if anyone chose to leave his church, he would pray they would get Cancer. As unbelievable as this sounds, I really didn't care about these revelations because I was so wounded from what had happened to me in the church foyer. Nothing they said changed my mind about the church. If anything, it fuelled my reasons for leaving. The wolf in sheep's clothing had spiritually pulled my family apart and it was too late to put our dismembered parts back together now.

Thankfully, my parents slowly recovered and found healing in another church. Nevertheless, God would have to wait a long time for my reconciliation. Damage from the shots the reverend had helped the hunter fire in the foyer after church had caused deep wounding and I was done with church, with Christianity, and with God. Now the hunter, Satan, had me right where he wanted me, wounded and on the run.

Who Hindered Your Running?

Unfortunately, I'm probably not the only one whose been subjected to that kind of verbal abuse from a leader in the church and most likely I will not be the last. You can be running so well with God until you start to believe in fake bugle calls, causing you to run in the opposite direction, finding yourself in a totally different place to where God intended you to be. In Galatians 5:7-9, Paul reminds the church of Galatia to walk in the freedom of the Spirit. 'You were running [the race] well; who has interfered and prevented you from obeying the truth? This [deceptive] persuasion is not from Him who called you [to freedom in Christ]. A little leaven [a slight inclination to error, or a few false teachers] leavens the whole batch [it perverts the concept of faith and misleads the church].[11] Paul was warning the church in Galatia that even a small amount of deceitful persuasion has a negative impact across the whole congregation if left unchecked. The behaviour from my parents revealed how bad the fungus from the reverend's false teaching had spread. God doesn't use deceptive bugle calls to get you to do what He wants you to do, that's the hunter, Satan's approach.

If you've been on the receiving end of verbal abuse from a leader and it's caused you run from the church, then I'm sorry. I'm sorry you felt shame as the shots the hunter, Satan, fired caused you to become so wounded. Or maybe like my parents, you watched something happen and never did anything about it because you were so confused from the fake bugle calls of the hunter you had no capacity to see the truth. Recovering from wounds caused by false teaching is a lengthy process and the danger is that you can shut yourself off from hearing any future bugle calls from God because the fake bugle calls of the hunter, Satan, have left you so wounded and so confused, you're now scared to act on the real bugle call that leads you back to the herd. The truth is that regardless of how many bad choices you've made or believe you've made, in spite of listening to every one of those fake bugle calls from the hunter, Satan, God's *real* bugle call still sounds out for your relationship with Him to be reconciled and restored.

The Heartbeat of God

For a long time, I didn't understand what the *'heartbeat of God'* meant. The shame of our rebellion keeps us hidden in the forest of pain as we try to fix up our wounds ourselves because every bugle call made us think it was the authentic voice of God. However, each one turned out to be the fake bugle call of the hunter, Satan, that left a blood trail from our wounds for him to track. Knowing this we kept hidden from God, closing ourselves off from His voice because we are too afraid to come out of hiding in case it's the wrong sound.

In the Old Testament when Israel heard the voice of God, they obeyed the law and listened to the message He sent through the prophets. The people who were in a covenant relationship with God knew the sound of His voice.[12] A covenant is a formal agreement between two people and binds them together. However, the responsibilities in keeping the covenant are honesty, sincerity, and good will. The heartbeat of God is the sound of these values which maintains the covenant relationship between us. Perhaps this is why Jesus gives the illustration of the Good Shepherd in John chapter 10 to the Pharisees? Circling back to the fact that His sheep know the sound of His voice because the Good Shepherd protects His sheep at all costs.

'I am the Good Shepherd. The Good Shepherd puts the sheep before himself, sacrifices himself if necessary. A hired man is not a real shepherd. The sheep mean nothing to him. He sees a wolf come and runs for it, leaving the sheep to be ravaged and scattered by the wolf. He's only in it for the money. The sheep don't matter to him. I am the Good Shepherd. I know my own sheep and my own sheep know me. In the same way, the Father knows me, and I know the Father. I put the sheep before myself, sacrificing myself if necessary. You need to know that I have other sheep in addition to those in the pen. I need to gather and bring them too; They'll also recognise my voice.'[13]

Quieten your mind and focus on the Good Shepherd's voice, the real bugle call that carries the sound of His heartbeat. Stop running for just a moment and attune your ears again to the safe sound of His voice and you'll start to hear a faint whisper. Don't be scared. Don't be tempted to run again, just take notice of the sound of the bugle call until it starts to become clearer. A real bugle call doesn't sound like an accusation. It doesn't torment you with the mistakes you've made. It never sounds out its manipulation into your thinking or hurls abuse at you. The sound of a real bugle call from the Good Shepherd has a different tone to it. A heavenly melody that calls you into restoration, into rescue, into love.

Listen carefully because He's calling you…

Endnotes: Chapter Three

Ref 1   Youtube Video. 'You will recover all.' Bill Johnson (full sermon) Bethel Church Jan 8th 2022.

Ref 2   8 facinating facts about elk By Tyler Wilcox May 2019

Ref 3   elk101.com/2016/03/why-do-elk-bugle-and-run/ (Elk101)

Ref 4   reelgamecalls.com/elk-bugle-secrets-tips/

Ref 5   Habakkuk 2:2-3 *Amplified Holy Bible: Captures the Full Meaning behind the Original Greek and Hebrew.* 2015. Grand Rapids, Michigan: Zondervan.

Ref 6   Desilva, David Arthur. 2018. *An Introduction to the New Testament: Contexts, Methods & Ministry Formation.* Downers Grove, Illinois: Ivp Academic, An Imprint Of InterVarsity Press.   Page 887, Alphacrucis College Library.

Ref 7   John 10:4 *Amplified Holy Bible: Captures the Full Meaning behind the Original Greek and Hebrew.* 2015. Grand Rapids, Michigan: Zondervan.

Ref 8   Outdoorhub.com (website)

Ref 9   livingwithwolves.org./how-wolves-hunt/

Ref 10   Matthew 7:15 *Amplified Holy Bible: Captures the Full Meaning behind the Original Greek and Hebrew.* 2015. Grand Rapids, Michigan: Zondervan.

Ref 11   Galatians 5:7-9 *Amplified Holy Bible: Captures the Full Meaning behind the Original Greek and Hebrew.* 2015. Grand Rapids, Michigan: Zondervan.

Ref 12   Keener, Craig S. 1993. *The IVP Bible Background Commentary: New Testament.* Downers Grove, Ill. InterVarsity Press.

Ref 13   John 10:11-15 Peterson, Eugene H. 2000. *The Message Bible:* Colorado Springs, Colorado. Navpress.

CHAPTER FOUR

Leaving a Blood Trail

'As soon as her fingers brushed His cloak, the bleeding stopped.'[1]
MARK 5:29

'He's tall, handsome and in the Navy and he'd like to meet you.' The words from my matchmaker friend's lips caused a rush of excitement, mingled with fear all at the same time within me. Why would someone like him what to meet someone like me? Sunday morning came and my friend was late picking me up. Really late. This gave room for mum's regular Christian pep talk before heading off to church with dad. Mum was trying to convince me that going to church rather than a theme park on a Sunday with my friend, her boyfriend and her boyfriend's mysterious sailor friend, was the better option for my eternity. But, like they say, curiosity always killed the cat, and as I closed the front door on my mother's glares that morning and headed toward my friend's boyfriend's car, my curiosity to meet the tall, handsome sailor overrode my mum's pleas for me to return to church.

An Unclean Outcast

'God's love is towards you, and you know, you've actually needed that love and it's almost like you've been starved of it for a while' the words from the prophesy were the truth. I had been starved from lack of affirmation, longing to hear the words, 'I love you' just once from my parents growing up, as I struggled with my insecurities of not fitting in, of never being enough, of feeling unclean and thinking I was an outcast. The hunter, Satan, knew the total disregard for my feelings from the abuse I received from the reverend months earlier would open old abandonment wounds and stop the seed of the prophetic words taking root into my heart. The penetrating shots the reverend had helped the hunter, Satan, fire, reminded me of those all too familiar feelings of shame and humiliation from the bullying and name-calling I had encountered a couple of years earlier at school when I was struggling to manage my bladder issues, and one day in P.E. I laughed too hard and wet myself in front of the class, resulting in a horrendous year of bullying in school.

For many years I have felt too ashamed to speak about my hidden secret. Enuresis is a condition that causes bedwetting, and even though my mum tried to help me, the doctors could find nothing physically wrong with me or my bladder function. I was five years old when my struggle to stay dry for at least one night started to become a problem. Trying to manage the problems that go along with enuresis as a teenager are difficult to control. The shame and embarrassment that come with the condition made me want to hide my issues from everyone, plus the emotional toll on my fragile self-esteem caused trauma.

Suffering Greatly

Whenever I read about the woman who had suffered 12 years from a condition that left her unclean and an outcast in Mark chapter 5, I become emotional. I completely identify with how she's feeling. Although I suffered from a different condition to this woman, my brokenness and suffering didn't need more abuse hurled at it, it needed a touch from Jesus.

'In the crowd pressing around Jesus, there was a woman who had suffered continuous bleeding for 12 years, bleeding that made her ritually unclean and an outcast according to the purity laws. She had suffered greatly; and although she spent all her money on her medical care, she had only gotten worse. She had heard of this Miracle-Man, Jesus, so she snuck up behind Him in the crowd and reached out her hand to touch His cloak. (To herself) Even if all I touch are His clothes, I know I will be healed. As soon as her fingers brushed His cloak, the bleeding stopped. She could feel that she was whole again. Lots of people were pressed against Jesus at that moment, but He immediately felt her touch; He felt healing power flow out of Him. He stopped. Everyone stopped. He looked around. 'Who touched My robe?' His disciples broke the uneasy silence. 'Jesus, the crowd is so thick that everyone is touching You. Why do You ask, 'Who touched Me?' But Jesus waited. His gaze swept across the crowd to see who had done it. At last, the woman – knowing He was talking about her – pushed forward and dropped to her knees. She was shaking with fear and amazement. 'I touched You.' Then she told Him the reason why. Jesus listened to her story. 'Daughter, you are well because you dared to believe. Go in peace and stay well.' [2]

Trauma wounds can make us feel like an unclean outcast, impacting the shame we're feeling from our *continuous bleeding* that can keep us running. Looking back on this time in my life, I think the majority of my healing came because the doctor who helped me become dry every night understood the psychological effects my bedwetting had caused me. For the first time in my life, I felt heard as he just listened to my story, just like the woman who had been healed from her continuous bleeding, Jesus listened to her story. I truly believe that healing for some of our wounding can come when someone just listens to our story, I mean really listens to our story. And I also believe, even though I'd abandoned God, the church, and my Christianity, it was during those months of phone calls I had unknowingly brushed my fingers against Jesus' cloak, and He was asking, 'who touched Me?'. However, more healing needed to come before I was ready to stop running from God, the church, and my past.

Hiding Becomes Survival

There's a rumour circling my family that because we moved around a lot when I was a kid, my mum could possibly be a descendent of Irish travellers. So, I guess running could definitely be in my blood, right?! Perhaps that's why years later, I ended up marrying the tall, handsome sailor I met that Sunday morning, and I found myself running away to Portsmouth with him, leaving all my past behind me in the town I grew up in and start a new life as a Naval wife. Six years later we felt the pull to adventure again and this time we made plans to move to the other side of the world. We landed at Sydney airport in the

September of 2001, with our two children, four suitcases and a heart full of dreams. Just two days later we saw the tragedy of 9/11 in New York unfold and we believed that Philip would be requested to do a 'Return of Service' as it is an obligation when you leave employment of Her Majesty's Defence Force. The anxious wait on whether Philip was going to be called back to the Navy was over after a letter came a couple of weeks later stating he would not be asked to return to duties because of his 'geographical location'.

Looking back in retrospect on that inner boldness we possessed, the courage and determination to move our little family twelve thousand miles away from everything that felt familiar, I realise now, how much of a sacrifice it was for Philip to leave his career in the British Navy so he could give his children a more fulfilling life in Australia. And even though Philip didn't believe in Christianity, and I had abandoned God and the church because of wounding, I can honestly say that no one can ever outrun God, because God still operates His redemption plan to steer the trajectory of our path toward a future that He planned for us, even in the hiding.

For me, perhaps the driving motive of moving towns and then countries, is that nobody knows anything about you. You can start again, reinvent yourself, and leave out all those yucky details about your past behind. New friends you meet twelve thousand miles from the town you grew up in don't know that you laughed too hard in P.E. one day when you were thirteen, causing you to wet yourself in front of all your classmates, which left you humiliated, bullied, and ashamed by the whole school for the rest of the school year. New relationships don't prod as to why you and your best friend when you were both fourteen, hid behind a bush in a street one night because you were both drunk, and watched a police car drive by, hoping the policemen didn't see you. They don't question why you were the rebellious teenager who wanted so desperately to fit in and thought that underaged drinking was what the cool kids did. People don't really care if you abandoned your relationship with God and gave up on going to church when you were fifteen because of verbal abuse from a reverend. And they shall never understand the truth as to why you secretly had an abortion when you were almost seventeen. Moving around and constantly hiding becomes your survival when you've been wounded and are on the run because of your past mistakes.

Survival Mode

Hiding is survival for an elk who is wounded and, on the run, too. Any blood spots, or hoof prints are clues for the hunter to track the elk down. The hunter knows that the wounded elk is out there somewhere, hiding in the trees and scrub, so with the help of GPS, the hunter is able to track the wounded animal by dropping a pin on the map where blood is found on tree branches or grass as this helps locate the direction the wounded elk is heading.

Elks have incredible senses to protect themselves from danger. Large ears are beneficial to strange noises and eyes positioned on the sides of their head help them to distinguish movement, along with a great sense of smell,[3] so the hunter needs to be patient and have the endurance to follow the blood trail which will lead him straight to the elk.

While researching blood trailing, I found that many hunters gain a sense of accomplishment by how many points a downed elk has on its antlers. The ranking system is, an elk with a total of twelve antler points (6x6) is called a 'royal bull', one with fourteen antler points (7x7) is called an 'imperial', and a sixteen antler point elk (8x8) is called a 'monarch'. [4] These stately names given to elk's that have the highest number of points on their antlers, show that no matter how hard the elk tries to hide and recover from its wounding, the hunter knows that the more antler points the elk has, the more it's a prize worth having.

Let me share a revelation with you that I've learned over my years of running and hiding because of shameful wounds from my past. If you've accepted Jesus into your heart, no amount of running or hiding can change the fact that you're marked with God's seal.

> Your lives are marked with His seal.

You can move towns, cities or even emigrate to another country across the world, but it does not alter the fact that you are a child of God. Paul states this fact in Ephesians 1:13, 'Because you, too, have heard the word of truth – the good news of your salvation – and because you believed in the One who is truth, your lives are marked with His seal.' [5] Whether you're a 'royal bull' an 'imperial' or a 'monarch', the rack on your head that you've tried to cover up and hide from people, doesn't stop or deter the hunter, Satan, from pursuing you because he knows you're a prize worth having.

Remembering part of the prophesy spoken over me when I was fifteen, God said that He wanted me to hear His heartbeat, He wanted me to experience intimacy with Him. Intimacy? What did that mean exactly? To be honest, I was scared, and I believe the word 'intimacy' scared the hunter, Satan too because he knew that was the moment, the signal for him to start disassembling any chance of an intimate relationship between myself and God. Why? Because Satan understands that intimacy between us and God brings a confidence in knowing who we are and Whose we are. It settles down our troubled souls when we battle with our insecurities and struggle with our fears. We don't need to hide from God because of our wounding when we have an intimate relationship with Him because we have the confidence that we're worthy enough of His healing love. We can come out from hiding under the shadow of the forest trees and live in the wide, open space of our inheritance.

Up until now, you may have been unaware that if you have 'believed in the One who is truth' then you are marked with God's seal. I hid the real me for years, hoping to fit in, believing that if I kept out of church then the royal seal of God would be hidden and somehow disappear. Believe it or not, it does not matter how far you have run or how long you've been hiding from God, His seal upon you is still visible in the spiritual realm and is glaringly obvious to the hunter, Satan.

This is why he hunts you down so furiously, making sure those festering wounds bleed out so you feel you cannot have an intimate relationship with God. The hunter, Satan needs your wounds to keep bleeding out so he can follow the blood trail that will lead him to you. Perhaps when I mentioned intimacy with God earlier, you felt it wasn't right, it wasn't proper. Intimacy is between lovers, not God and us! However, trust comes through an intimate relationship, and this is why Satan needs to keep us wounded and, on the run, so that the trusting bond between us and God, cannot be formed.

Synonyms of the word 'intimacy' are affection, confidence, friendship, familiarity, and understanding.[6] This is why you've been hurt so badly by the hunter, Satan. He designed each arrow tip so that they seep toxins into your thinking. Poison left untended keeps wounds of not feeling worthy enough of having an intimate relationship with God fresh and raw, so you'll never allow Him to get close enough to heal you, causing you to rank yourself as a beggar rather than as royalty. Satan knows this infected thinking will blight the royal seal of approval that was bestowed upon you by the King of Kings and keep you in a perpetual cycle of believing God will never be there to support you.

From That Day Forward

In the book of 1 Samuel, we see the story unfold of a young shepherd boy named, David, who was anointed with oil by the prophet, Samuel, to become the next king of Israel, taking over the reign of King Saul. Saul loved David so much that he became Saul's armourbearer and commander of his army. Even Saul's son, Johnathan, loved David so abundantly that he gave him his armour, symbolizing that he was transferring his birthright of becoming king to David. The trajectory of God's promise on David's life seemed to be going in the right direction. However, King Saul's love for David turned sour because he allowed his insecurities to consume his thinking.

'As they were coming [home], when David returned from killing the Philistine, the women came out of all the cities of Israel, singing and dancing, to meet king Saul with tambourines, [songs of] joy, and musical instruments. The women sang as they played and danced saying, 'Saul has slain his thousands, and David his ten thousands.' Then Saul became very angry, for this saying displeased him; and he said, 'They have ascribed to David ten thousands, but to me they have ascribed [only] thousands. Now what more can he have but the kingdom?' Saul looked at David with suspicion [and jealously] from that day forward.' [7] (1 Samuel 18:6-9)

Saul's obsessive pursuit over David's demise caused David to eventually run and hide. Instead of seeing the anointing over David's life as a credit and a benefit to his own reign as king, Saul allowed the bitter roots of his insecurities to wreck a great friendship. All the same, the seal of God wasn't erased just because David was in hiding. And before you start scratching at those wounds that remind you that you're not as perfect as David, his life was littered with mistakes. Nevertheless, God never withdrew His seal from him, and He won't remove His seal from you either. Sometimes hiding can be used by God to draw us closer to Him, but only if we allow Him to minister to our wounded souls. Although David was wounded by Saul's careless behaviour, he sought God even in his hidden state. David wrote two wonderful Psalms in the caves where he hid. The first is Psalm 57 and the second is Psalm 142. Let's read them together.

> Psalm 57
> 'Be good to me God -and now!
> I've run to you for dear life.
> I'm hiding out under your wings
> Until the hurricane blows over.
> I call out to High God,
> the God who holds me together.
> He sends orders from heaven and saves me,

he humiliates those who kick me around.
God delivers generous love,
He makes good on his word.

I find myself in a pride of lions
who are wild for a taste of human flesh;
Their teeth are lances and arrows,
their tongues are sharp daggers.

Soar high in the skies, O God!
Cover the whole earth with your glory!

They booby-trapped my path;
I thought I was dead and done for.
They dug a mantrap to catch me,
and fell in headlong themselves.

I'm ready, God, so ready,
Ready from head to toe,
Ready to sing, ready to raise a tune:
'Wake up, harp! wake up, lute!
Wake up, you sleepyhead sun!'

I'm thanking you, God, out loud in the streets,
singing your praises in town and country.
The deeper your love, the higher it goes;
every cloud is a flag to your faithfulness.

Soar high in the skies, O God!
Cover the whole earth with your glory![8]

Psalm 142.
'I cry out loudly to God,
loudly I plead with God for mercy.
I spill out all my complaints before him,
and spell out my troubles in detail:

'As I sink in despair, my spirit ebbing away,
you know how I'm feeling,
Know the danger I'm in,
the traps hidden in my path.
Look right, look left –
there's not a soul who cares what happens!
I'm up against it, with no exit –
bereft, left alone.
I cry out, God, call out:
'You're my last chance, my only hope for life!'
Oh listen, please listen;
I've never been this low.
Rescue me from those who are hunting me down;
I'm no match for them.
Get me out of this dungeon
so I can thank you in public.
Your people will form a circle around me
and you'll bring me showers of blessing!'[9]

The one quality I love about David's character is that he didn't allow the hunter's arrows to wound him to the point that it disabled his intimate relationship with God. He kept communicating with God in his hiding even though his circumstances looked nothing like God had promised. He kept reminding himself of Who God was, even when he was wounded by the actions of Saul. And because of David's obedience, God used those times of covering to develop an even greater intimacy in his relationship with the man whom He had anointed as the next king of Israel.

So, When Do You Come Out of Hiding?

Regrettably, I didn't give God a chance when I was a teenager to reconcile my relationship with Him. I hid because I had allowed the foolishness of the reverend's actions to wound me so badly that it seeped poison into my soul, which caused the intimacy God longed for to lay dormant for years. Resentment toward me could have been the reason why the reverend was so venomous when he verbally abused me in the foyer after church? Who can tell? However, one thing is for certain, the hunter, Satan, isn't shy in leveraging other believer's insecurities to wound you so terribly that it causes you to hide who you truly are in Christ. Sadly, this wasn't the one and only time I allowed the jealousy of another believer to cause me to hide who I was, but I'll save that story for a later chapter.

So, the question remains, when is it safe to come out of hiding when the hunter, Satan, has a target on your back because of the royal seal of God marked on your head? When you feel that ache in your soul that you can't get rid of no matter how hard you try and hide it. When you sense that you won't get any real satisfaction in this life unless you come out of hiding and return back to Him.

Thirteen years was how long David hid in caves from Saul. Thirteen! Ironically, this was the same amount of time for me when I decided that I was going to act upon the whisperings of

God's bugle call and return, if somewhat apprehensively, to Him, to the Church, to my calling. Unbeknown to anyone, I had quietly recommitted my life to Jesus just before moving out to Australia. Mum always insisted on giving me one of her devotional booklets that had a salvation prayer in between its pages, and I decided one day to say it. Not only that, but she also continued to pray for mine and my sister's salvation no matter how far we seemed to be away from God. Let me assure you, the hunter, Satan, hasn't a hope in hell of keeping you from mending your broken relationship with God if you have a praying mother! However, regardless of my recommitment, I still chose to do nothing about the promise God had given me. I still decided that returning to church was just the next move toward God I wasn't prepared to do.

All that said, it was two years after we'd purchased a block of land and built our new house, that mum and dad decided to take the trip from England and visit their grandkids, who were now aged seven and three. During their visit, they asked if I could drive them to a local church one Sunday morning. I wasn't too fazed by this request, and I seem to recall Philip telling me to leave the kids at home with him. I decided that rather than drive all the way back home and then drive back to the church to pick up my parents, I would sit with them in the service.

Old memories of growing up in church came flooding back in my mind as I listened to the preacher. After the service refreshments were served and pleasantries were made. Mum tends to overshare, especially when she's chatting with new people, which meant half the church members practically knew everything about my family by the time we said our goodbyes. My plan was to stay hidden, guarded, and quiet, but clearly mum's annoying habit of oversharing dismantled any walls I was trying to build.

For some unknown reason, after my parents returned back to England again, I decided to come out of my hiding place and seek the intimacy God had asked me for thirteen years previously. Within a couple of months, myself and my kids had made friends with some of the congregational members of the church my parents had attended. I told Philip, that myself and the kids were going to be attending the church each week and he wasn't too keen on the idea. I remember him saying to me, 'I won't stop you and the kids going if that's what you want to do, but don't ever ask me to come along because I'll never set foot in that place. Understand?' Even though I had friends at the church, part of me still felt alone at times because I wasn't able to really share with my husband how 'awakened' I felt from rekindling my relationship with God. Blissfully unaware the enemy was tracking the drops of blood I was leaving behind from the hidden wounds from my past, it wouldn't be long before he lined up his scope to fire at me again.

I'm getting ahead of myself again telling you my story, but I want to take a moment to encourage someone in case they have heard enough about wounding and decide to leave this cabin they've found in the forest and start running again. My husband became a Christian many years after the grand announcement of never going to church and has now become a kingdom builder; meaning he is passionate about mentoring and discipling people who make up God's church. I am still amazed at how God turned his life completely around. Trust me when I say that no one is

> **Don't give up... God is still in the business of miracles.**

ever too hidden for God to find. And if you have been praying, if you've been standing in the gap for the salvation of your husband, your wife, your kids, or the lady on the checkout in your local supermarket, don't give up on them because God is still in the business of miracles.

I'm such an advocate of prayer. Prayer is so important because it covers us as we take this journey toward freedom from being blood trailed by the hunter, Satan. After each of the four parts along this journey to your wounds turning into valuable scars, I have written a prayer to help in your healing process. Feel free to say your own prayer or use my prayer as a guide to start you off as you rekindle and rebuild your relationship with Jesus again.

PRAYER

Dear Jesus,
I ask You to help heal the wounds where my trust has been violated because of the abuse of people who were in authority over me within the church. Comfort me in the painful memories of what happened to me and help me to trust You enough to show You my wounds, and allow You, Jesus, to turn them into valuable scars. I have been wounded so badly that I find it hard to trust people and so I run and hide out of fear of being hurt again. But I now understand that I don't need to hide my wounds from You, I just need to tell You my story, like the woman with the issue of blood. I don't need to run anymore because of my fearful emotions. Restore me Jesus where I have blamed myself for the bad choices I've made in my past. Free me from the shame I have felt and

wrap me in the warmth of Your embrace. Help me, Jesus, to find a good mentor, someone I can trust fully for future guidance and instruction in Your ways. I know now that You love me, and You always have, and I am sorry for believing the lies of the hunter, Satan, who told me that You don't care about my wounds. Forgive me, restore me, cleanse me from my past. Amen.

Endnotes: Chapter Four

Ref 1 (Quote) Mark 5:29 Ecclesia Bible Society. 2012. *The Voice Bible: Step into the Story of Scripture.* Nashville: Thomas Nelson.

Ref 2 Mark 5:24-34 Ecclesia Bible Society. 2012. *The Voice Bible: Step into the Story of Scripture.* Nashville: Thomas Nelson.

Ref 3 Sciencetrek.org Elk: facts (science Trek: Idaho Public Television)

Ref 4 Wapititalk.com/Rating System/Ranking System.

Ref 5 Ephesians 1:13 Ecclesia Bible Society. 2012. *The Voice Bible: Step into the Story of Scripture.* Nashville: Thomas Nelson.

Ref 6 Thesaurus. com

Ref 7 1 Samuel 18:6-9 *Amplified Holy Bible: Captures the Full Meaning behind the Original Greek and Hebrew.* 2015. Grand Rapids, Michigan: Zondervan.

Ref 8 Psalm 57, Peterson, Eugene H. 2000. *The Message Bible:* Colorado Springs, Colorado. Navpress.

Ref 9 Psalm 142, Peterson, Eugene H. 2000. *The Message Bible:* Colorado Springs, Colorado. Navpress.

PART TWO

THE RUT

CHAPTER FIVE

Dangerous Territory

'Sometimes the idea of living as a hermit appeals to all of us. No demands, no needs, no pain, no disappointments. But that is because we have been hurt, are worn out.'[1]
STASI ELDREDGE

Elk calves are especially vulnerable to predators and need protection for the first few weeks of life. Female elks (cows) will leave the herd when they're ready to give birth. Hiding her young calf is her top priority and vitally important toward its survival against passing predators. Thankfully, the calf's camouflage made up of cream-coloured spots along their back helps keep it hidden in thick grasses where the mother leaves the motionless calf for a while so she can find food. However, the cow cannot leave her young calf for too long as there could be wolves, bears, coyotes or bobcats, and these expert hunters are always on the prowl for an easy meal. Amazingly, an elk calf does not produce any odour, making it harder for a predator to sniff the calf out of its hidden location.[2] To make sure there is no evidence of the birth, the female cow will lick her calf clean and eat the placenta to deter any opportunity for a predator to strike.[3]

Although I had the basic, foundational beliefs of Christianity from growing up in church, I was still a newborn in many ways spiritually. Re-joining a herd of believers when you've ran for so long from them takes time to figure out where you fit in and whether you'll be accepted. The years of running had made me weak and in need of spiritual nourishment, so I was pleased there was a small library of Christian books in the church to borrow from as I didn't have any religious books in my bookshelf at home.

The petite lady with the halo of tightly permed grey hair and smiling eyes was responsible for writing down who borrowed which book and the date it needed to be returned. Intrigued by my desire to read as much as I could about God, she commented one Sunday morning while I was scanning the bookshelves. 'You know, you're my best customer,' she chuckled, 'Normally nobody ever comes in here.' I frowned, 'Really? There's so many great books in here! Do you have any recommendations?' My question caused a sparkle to run through her smiling eyes, and she proceeded to highlight a few favourites of hers.

I was spiritually starving and hungry to know more about God as I devoured each book she was recommending. Regardless of leaving out a few ugly details about my past in our regular library conversations, she could clearly see the leader I was trying to keep hidden and encouraged me to share book reviews on the books I'd been reading with the congregation to promote the church library. I'd been attending the church for a while by now and so we decided to pitch the idea to one of the elders. Amazingly, the elder said if the pastor was happy with me giving a book review now and again in the service then I could do it.

My five-minute book review each month started to become one of the highlights for the congregation and progressed to me reading my own short stories each week which I'd started to write. They even found a comfortable reading chair for me to sit in as a 'set design' for my segment in the service. After a few months, my library friend quietly commented one day on my contribution to the service. She had that sparkle in her eyes again as she leaned in and whispered to me, 'I know you write short stories for the children to listen to, but I learn more about Jesus from you than I do from the preaching.'

As I felt my own faith being rebirthed, I watched my children's faith slowly develop too as we started doing life with seasoned believers. Unfortunaly, even after a few years of myself and my kids attending church, my husband still didn't want to be a part of it. He was happy to meet with my friends in their houses but refused to come to the church. Even though I felt safe in the herd of believers, with no spiritual covering from my husband, I was in dangerous territory as the odour from my wounding started to leak out.

Seeking affirmation from people instead of God became the driving force for me to serve in church and my low self-esteem and vulnerability made me an easy target for the hunter, Satan. However, I loved teaching truths about Jesus and sharing my revelations to the congregation and it seemed all those drama sketches I was a part of while growing up in church helped me to not be fearful of public speaking. Nevertheless, regardless of how cleaned up my life felt, my lack of awareness of the infection developing from my past wound of abandonment and the odour seeping out of my emotional need to feel accepted and approved caused me to become reckless, unguarded, and naïve. Like an elk calf attempting to run on fresh, unsteady legs too soon, I was trying to run on my 'spiritual' wobbly legs before I was taught how to properly walk with God and get my affirmation from Him.

After a few years of patiently waiting in the shadows, watching my movements, the hunter, Satan, leveraged the absence of spiritual covering from my husband and used this void as an opportune moment to search his arsenal of weaponry to start another blood trail. His weapon of choice this time? An arrow that would be dipped into the poison of betrayal and he would aim it straight at my heart.

The Wound

Living with a husband who works shifts is hard when you have two young children, so I spent many hours around my friends' houses from church just so Philip could get enough sleep and wouldn't be disturbed by the kids. Some friends feel like family, but the danger is if our need for them is rooted in the wounds from our past, then a blood trail will be inevitable.

One afternoon I visited my good friends and after a while, I could sense something wasn't right. My friend seemed preoccupied with her kids in another room while I was chatting with her husband. I didn't have my kids with me on this occasion and I was glad of that fact because out of the blue, my friend's husband took a deep breath and said he had something to tell me, and he just couldn't keep in in any longer. My mind raced as I wondered what it was. Was my friend, ok? Did they need my help? By the awkwardness on his face, I felt a little nervous to what he was going to say. But I decided to wait patiently for him to speak before my thoughts ran away with me. He took another deep breath and finally said, 'I've struggled to tell you this and I've wrestled with it for a while. I want you to know that I've dealt with it now, but I just can't hold it in any longer.' Pausing again, he looked at me and said, 'I need to confess that I had fallen in love with you. I've told my wife, I've dealt with it, and I'm no longer in love with you now.' After this confession, I just stood there stunned and eventually rambled, 'But you're good now, right?' Just so the uncomfortable moment would pass. I didn't know what else to do or how to react. My first thought was I needed to get out of there as quickly as possible, but my friend came back into the room again and she said, 'So he's told you?' All I could do was nod to her. The minutes that followed felt strange and very uncomfortable and were filled with more awkward conversation. I told them I really needed to go, and I'd see them another time. When I arrived home, I mistakenly decided not to tell my husband what had just occurred as I was trying to process everything that had just happened myself.

 A few weeks went by, and I felt that the best thing to do was to write a letter to my friend's husband and explain why I was declining his offers via text to go over for a visit to their house. My hand-written note was raw and honest, and I explained that I was heartbroken because I knew my friendship with his wife would have to come to an end. I thought the letter would help him understand how I felt about his confession to me, and I told him it would be best for everyone if we just parted ways. A couple of weeks later, I received a typed, official-looking letter stating that I was making everything up and he was threating legal action. I was in total shock. I knew I needed to show my husband the letter and tell him everything that had happened.

Dangerous Territory

The months that followed were the hardest in my marriage. I felt as though I had lost everything and the only thing that I could cling onto was my integrity as Philip was trying to understand why I didn't tell him what had happened. He was deeply hurt, and he felt as though I didn't trust him. We were in a rut, and even though I had been a Navel wife and was used to being apart from my husband, the very foundation at the start of our marriage had been built on trust. So, why was I so afraid to tell him my secret? My only explanation was that I had been praying for so long for him to find redemption that I thought if I told him what had happened, he would step into the dangerous territory of losing his salvation forever.

> Rather than allowing God to cultivate our identity in Him first, we cloak our wounds in an identity that relies on something other than Him.

However, I was the one who had mistakenly roamed into dangerous territory because I had attached my identity to my Christian friends and how many church activities, I could be involved in to try to please Jesus. Ann Voskamp in her book, *The Broken Way* addresses this problem when she said, 'the core of every one of our issues is this attempt to construct our identity on something else besides Christ'. [4] Wounds caused by abandonment can lead us into more wounding because we start to build our identity in people and the things we do for God. This can lead us into dangerous territory as we take our first wobbly steps in our faith. Rather than allowing God to cultivate our identity in Him first, we cloak our wounds in an identity that relies on something other than Him.

Although painful, God in His mercy and grace will allow us to wonder into dangerous territory just so we are stripped of the false identity we have made from our wounding.

The only way I knew how to fight for my marriage was to get into my prayer closet. I had to believe that God would show everyone that the accusations against me were false, and the lies and gossip being spread about me were totally untrue. And yet, in the weeks of heartache and loneliness, in the blood trail of my brokenness that had led the hunter, Satan to discover me once again, I felt closer to God than I ever had before.

Position Yourself

In 2 Chronicles 20:17 Jahaziel the son of Zechariah told Judah, Jerusalem, and king Jehoshaphat that they would not need to fight because the battle was the Lord's. 'You will not need to fight in this battle. Position yourselves, stand still and see the salvation of the Lord, who is with you, O Judah and Jerusalem! Do not fear or be dismayed; tomorrow go out against them, for the Lord is with you.' [5] When you position yourself in a posture of prayer, you're letting the hunter, Satan know that even though you're in dangerous territory, you have the covering of God for your survival. As a female elk protects her inexperienced young calf who doesn't see that they've wondered unknowingly into dangerous territory, God will protect His children by teaching them how to hide *in* Him.

Hiding *in* God is completely different to hiding *from* Him when we are wounded and on the run. Psalm 91:1-3 reminds us that we are safe and secure from the hunter when we choose to hide ourselves in God. 'When you sit enthroned under the shadow of Shaddai, you are hidden in the strength of God Most High. He's the hope that holds me and the Stronghold to shelter me, the only God for me, and my great confidence. He will rescue you from every hidden trap of the enemy, and he will protect you from false accusation and any deadly curse.'[6]

> **When you position yourself in a posture of prayer, you're letting the hunter, Satan know that even though you're in dangerous territory, you have the covering of God for your survival.**

Interestingly, the Hebrew word for deadly curse can mean 'poisoned arrows'[7] which is why we need to stay still and stay hidden under God's covering, so the arrow from the hunter won't take us out. When Jahaziel the son of Zechariah said that they'll see the salvation of the Lord, he was prophesying restoration and deliverance from the battle.

Where Is My Identity Found?

What about you, dear friend? Have your wounds caused you to cloak your identity in something other than God? Joseph is best known for the distinct coat his father gave to him to show he was the favoured son. This gesture angered his brothers so fiercely that they stripped him of the special coat, sold him into slavery to the Ishmaelites, and lied to their father, Jacob, telling him that Joseph was dead. The next time a garment of Joseph's is stripped from him is in Genesis 39. Potiphar was an officer of Pharaoh and he brought Joseph from the Ishmaelites to serve in his household. Potiphar clearly saw that God was with Joseph and he eventually put him in charge of everything he owned.

The Bible doesn't comment on Joseph's emotional wounding from the actions of his brothers. However, commentary suggests that the part in Joseph's story where he is serving in Potiphar's house has a common theme and could be leaning toward a rivalry between brothers. Like the story of Jacob and Esau, the relationship between Potiphar and Joseph could have possibly developed into a kind of brotherhood trust.[8] Perhaps Joseph was trying to cover his wound of abandonment from his brothers with an identity found in Potiphar's friendship? We shall never know, but one thing is clear, someone was impressed with Joseph, and she was ready to make her move.

'Now Joseph was handsome and attractive in form and appearance. Then after a time his master's wife looked at Joseph with desire, and she said, 'Lie with me.' But he refused and said to his master's wife, 'Look, with me in the house, my master does not concern himself with anything; he has put everything that he owns in my charge. He is not greater in this house than I am, nor has he kept anything from me except you, because you are his wife. How then could I do this great evil and sin against God [and your husband]?' (Genesis 39:6-9 Amp)

Garments in the ancient world were often given to indicate your status, rank, or office.⁸ Joseph's special cloak was stripped from him when his brothers sold him into slavery, now Joseph was about to have another identity stripped from him. 'Then it happened one day that Joseph went into the house to attend to his duties, and none of the men of the household was there in the house. She caught Joseph by his [outer] robe, saying, 'Lie with me!' But he left his robe in her hand and ran and got outside [the house].' (Genesis 39:11-12 Amp)

When you're emotionally damaged from the wounds of your past, the last thing you want to do is to create more wounding. I knew my friend's husband's confession to me wasn't something I was willing to test by continuing on with the friendship, so I needed to leave it behind. Joseph had to leave his cloak behind too because he had possibly wrapped his identity in something other than God. When Potiphar's wife falsely accused Joseph of rape, the law stated that Joseph would be executed. However, Potiphar sent Joseph to the royal prison (probably because of their brotherly friendship) instead of a death sentence. But even in the dungeon of despair, God looked after Joseph by helping him with all his abandonment issues. When Joseph eventually became second in command from Pharoah because he was able to interpret Pharoah's dream, he knew his identity was found in God and nothing else. 'Then Pharoah removed his signet ring from his finger and slipped it on Joseph's hand. He outfitted him in robes of the best linen and put a gold chain around his neck.' (Genesis 41:42 The Message)

In the silence of the prison, Joseph had finally discovered his identity was in God and Him alone. Regardless of the promotional robes Pharoah gave to him, Joseph now knew who he really was. Even though these robes represented his status over the Egyptians, he didn't wrap his identity up in them.

Our True Identity

I won't lie to you, being stripped of something you've wrapped your identity in is painful and feels very much like a death sentence. Whatever it is; a friendship, a job, a title, or your rank, there's a grief that comes with it, there's a process of letting go. But God, in His mercy, knows that the *something* that you've wrapped your identity up in needs to be left behind so you're able to find your identity and purpose in Him. In the deafening silence of the dungeon, God was still with Joseph. And in the deafening silence of your pain of having to leave something behind, God is still with you.

> But God, in His mercy, knows that the *something* that you've wrapped your identity up in needs to be left behind so you're able to find your identity and purpose in Him.

The story of Joseph gives us comfort, knowing that God will never abandon us. However, if the sole purpose of Joseph's story was to become Pharoah's second in command and rule over Egypt, then the ending of his story wouldn't have had the same transforming power. It would have left a very shallow taste in the mouth of the reader. Sure, he was where God had promised he'd be when he had revealed his dream to his brothers all those years ago, but a wound still needed to be dealt with and Joseph knew that his issues of betrayal from his brothers would have to be cleansed by the healing balm of forgiveness.

It just so happened that the land of Canaan was in a severe famine and Joseph's brothers had to travel to Egypt to buy some grain. Joseph was in charge of the grain storehouse and when his brothers came to purchase some grain, he recognised them. Interestingly, it took Joseph a few more chapters and a lot of weeping for him to finally come to a point of forgiving his brothers for what they did to him, allowing the wound of betrayal to be completely healed. 'I am Joseph your brother whom you sold into Egypt. But don't feel badly, don't blame yourselves for selling me. God was behind it. God sent me here ahead of you to save lives.' (Genesis 45:4 The Message)

A New Herd

The overarching theme of Joseph's story is to show how powerful forgiveness is. When you recognise someone from your past many years later down one of the aisles in your local supermarket, it can pick at the scab of your wounding. I was sure my old friend hadn't seen me and so I quickly found the items I needed and pushed my trolley toward the checkout. Just as I was almost at the checkout, she came around one of the aisles and said my name. I tried to act surprised, but I knew that she knew that I had seen her earlier. She apologised for everything that had happened, knowing the lies that had been spread about my character and the false accusation that I'd made up the story that her husband had told me he'd fallen in love with me. She bravely asked for my forgiveness and said that she was so sorry how I had been treated. And just like Joseph, I was faced with a choice. Was I going to allow the wounds her husband had caused me to fester, or was I going to forgive? Long before I met my old friend in the supermarket, I had chosen the healing balm found in forgiveness.

    I thanked my old friend for her bravery, and I told her I had forgiven them both and moved on. I still chose not to have a relationship with her or her husband, even after her apology because I knew it wasn't the right thing to do for my marriage. I was settled in another church by that point. However, the road toward forgiveness wasn't easy and it took me and my husband a while to fully and completely forgive the deep wounding that they had caused within our marriage. Remember, my husband was not a Christian at this point, but like Joseph, I couldn't allow my identity to become cloaked in unforgiveness.

> **Forgiving a betrayal is not easy and perhaps the wound is too fresh, too raw for you to allow the healing balm of forgiveness to soothe it right now.**

    Where are you at right now dear friend? Have you allowed a cloak of something to cover your true identity? Forgiving a betrayal is not easy and perhaps the wound is too fresh, too raw for you to allow the healing balm of forgiveness to soothe it right now. I know. I understand. It's a process, but if you allow that wound to fester, the hunter, Satan will find that blood trail you're leaving behind and hunt you down again. Like the elk calf, survival is important in our faith from predators because God wants us to become all that He needs us to be, so we are able to help others who have found themselves in dangerous territory too. Seeking out another church can help when you've stepped into dangerous territory. However, the hunter, Satan is always ready to pull back his bow and fire another arrow. For myself, the arrow of betrayal was being lined up again. But this time it wasn't designed just to take only me out, but my whole family too.

Endnotes: Chapter Five

Ref 1   Eldredge, John, Eldredge, Stasi. 2005. *Captivating: Unveiling the Mystery of a Woman's Soul.* Nashville, Tennessee. Thomas Nelson.

Ref 2   the-wild-life-of-elk. Weebly. Com/elk calves.

Ref 3   naturallynorthidaho.com/2014/05calf-survival-dependent-on-hiding. (by Laura)

Ref 4   Voskamp, Ann. 2016. *The Broken Way: A Daring Path to the Abundant Life.* Grand Rapids, Michigan: Zondervan.

Ref 5   2 Chronicles 20:17 *Spiritual Warfare Bible.* 2012. Lake Mary, Florida, Charisma House

Ref 6   Psalm 91:1-3 *The Passion Translation: New Testament with Psalms, Proverbs, and Song of Songs, Second Edition.* Passion & Fire Ministries, Inc. BroadStreet Publishing: 2018.

Ref 7   *The Passion Translation: New Testament with Psalms, Proverbs, and Song of Songs, Second Edition.* Passion & Fire Ministries, Inc. BroadStreet Publishing: 2018.
Commentary/ Deadly curse/ Hebrew word meaning poisoned arrows. (Psalm 91.)

Ref 8   Walton, John H, Victor Harold Matthew, and Mark William Chavalas. 2000. *The IVP Bible Background Commentary: Old Testament.* Downers Grove, Ill. InterVarsity Press.

CHAPTER SIX

The Kill Zone

'For there to be a betrayal, there would have to been trust first.'[1]
SUZANNE COLLINS. THE HUNGER GAMES

Bow hunters prefer the weapon of an arrow to take down a bull elk rather than a bullet. Known as the 'kill zone' this critical knowledge in the hunter's preparation, even before he ventures out on a hunt, is vitally important because he only has a limited amount of time to find the area on the elk's body to shoot at. Around 22-inches (55.88 centimetres) by 17-inches (43.18 centimetres) is about the space for the hunter to aim his arrow where it will be most effective in taking down the elk. Elks need to be positioned correctly if the arrow is to hit the target zone which will give the hunter the best outcome of penetration.[2]

Amazingly, elk can recover from muscle wounds if a bone isn't broken, so an experienced hunter doesn't jump to any conclusions if they track an elk and find it laying still. At any moment a downed elk can find the strength to get up and run, leaving the hunter empty-handed even after all the time they have invested in tracking the wounded elk along the blood trail. Responsible hunters make every effort to finish off the elk after blood trailing it, so aiming at the lung or heart in the kill zone area of the animal is the right thing to do.[3]

When you have been badly wounded by the arrow of betrayal from a close friend, you somehow manage to find the strength to get back up on your feet again. Hidden under the shadow of Shaddai, the deadly curse of the poisoned arrow Satan fired, is removed, and cleaned by the One who is the secret to your strength. Wrapped within His massive arms that are full of faithfulness, He uses them as a shield to keep you from harm.[4]

Like the elk, the fatal wound you believed would kill your faith was just a muscle wound that was unable to penetrate enough to break your relationship with God. As your wounds start to heal, the blood trail thins out, making it harder for the hunter to track.

Patient Endurance

As I mentioned in a previous chapter, the elk is believed to be a spirit animal and its strength and stamina symbolize endurance and patience. [5] To be honest, I had to learn patience and endurance when it came to my husband's salvation. I found I was always trying to set him up and coax him into coming along to church related events. However, like the elk's excellent sense smell, he could detect the scent of an altar call from a mile away and declined my offers of attending church events frequently.

The day my husband accepted Jesus' invitation to come and follow Him wasn't some big, extravagant moment. It took many years and many divine appointments for my husband to get to a point where he was willing to stand with a pastor and pray the salvation prayer, making Jesus Lord and Saviour over his life and become part of His story. I had been praying continually for this moment with endurance and patience. I even did an Esther fast after reading she fasted for three days to find favour with King Ahasuerus (Esther 4:16) to let God know I wasn't sending up half-hearted prayers to His throne room, but some steadfast, tenacious, cry out for a breakthrough kind of prayers, letting Him know I was serious in seeing His glory revealed in my husband's salvation. The strength and stamina that was birthed in my faith during those years of intercessory prayer helped me recover from my wounding and the damage the hunter, Satan tried to inflict into my marriage with his arrow of treachery. He had failed to take me down and the blood trail he had been following to track me and take me out completely had dried up.

There were a few good years where all my family served in church together and we were flourishing in our faith even though we had gone through some tough seasons. Eventually, after serving in many roles within the church, I was offered a job as the Personal Assistant to the pastors. I loved this role because part of being in this position meant I was now invited to attend more leaders' events and sit under the teaching of some very prominent influencers. Finally, I could sense some forward movement in my faith instead of going around in circles. No longer hidden and living in isolation from the herd, I was enjoying life and socialising within the group of believers. Grazing on a steady diet of God's Word, I found all the nutrients needed to help grow a healthy coat around my faith.

A Small Door of Opportunity

Sometimes blood trailing an elk can take time and the hunter can become mentally and physically fatigued while trying to track the animal down, especially if the blood trail has dried up. To fuel motivation, the hunter needs to find the elk and finish what he started, so he's going to need as much strength, stamina, endurance, and patience as the elk has if he is to succeed in taking the elk down. Weighing up the options of whether to keep pursuing the wounded animal need careful consideration from the hunter and the possibility of finding the elk and hitting it right in the kill zone area becomes a very small door of opportunity that the hunter needs to grasp with both hands. Knowing I had recovered from previous arrows, Satan had shot at me, he needed to make sure he aimed right at the kill zone to take me down. His strength, stamina, endurance, and patience were going to bring him the prize of not only my head on his trophy wall, but a whole church of believers who thought they were safe within the herd.

The alert of the hunter setting up a kill zone to take us all down came one Sunday morning when a pastor from one of the other campus's came to preach instead of our own campus pastor. My good friends who were the assistant pastors at the time said that everything will be explained to myself after the service. We waited until the church emptied and the visiting pastor started to explain that my friends wanted me to be the first to know that our campus pastor had confessed to embezzling funds not just from our church but eight other campuses within the movement. I felt the arrow tip hit my heart with such force that I found it hard to breathe. As I listened to the pastors tell me the whole story of our pastor's confession, I felt numb and needed time to process what they were saying. Should I get angry? Forgive? Or should I run away from the herd again? Going home and telling my family what had happened would be one of the hardest things I'd ever had to do.

The next evening, I told my husband I needed to go and see the campus pastor and his wife to offer my support. The pastor sobbed right in front of me, hugged me, and begged for my forgiveness. As a family, we had spent the last few years doing life with the pastor and his family, and I was determined that the wounds of betrayal, unforgiveness and bitterness would not penetrate my wounded soul again. Their friendship meant more to me than what had happened. Besides after my last wounding I could forgive and as a church we could get through this. Right? However, the wise council of my friends reminded me that even though my gracious efforts in helping to mop up the blood from my pastor's wounds were very noble, the blood seeping out of my own wound from the kill zone arrow the hunter had shot at me needed urgent care and attention and it would be heathier for me and help my own wounding to heal if I chose to distance myself from the pastor and his family while they healed.

Parasites and Diseases

Apart from hunters wounding and blood trailing elks, parasites and diseases are another major enemy of these majestic creatures. Ticks and mites are common among elks, and they can become so infested with mites that the poor animal rubs itself raw up against the bark of trees until the elk's protective coat falls out. The combination of hypothermia and huge scabbing all over its skin eventually leads to an untimely death. Horseflies are another parasite that transmit diseases, bringing with them roundworms, lungworms, and arterial worms from the horsefly's savage bite.[6]

After the initial shock of trying to digest the devastating news about our campus pastor, I needed to collect my thoughts and join with the leadership in supporting the congregation in any way I could. I knew one of the senior pastor's was coming the next week and had the unenviable task of announcing the bad news to the whole congregation. At first, it felt as though the arrow had pierced the church in the kill zone. The hunter, Satan had indeed aimed straight for the heart of our congregation and had every intention of fatally wounding us all. And yet, this perhaps wasn't what almost wiped our church out. It was the subtle and yet steady infiltration of disease into that wounding of betrayal which, I believe, caused the most damage within the herd of believers. And as the months rolled on, we all tried to grapple with our own emotions within the leadership as well as trying to help families and individuals process what had happened through pastoral care and counselling. It was all so emotionally draining and to add to the tension we knew if the news broke out into the community about our pastor's moral failure, our ideology of who we were as a church would carry no weight.

The Tree Bark of Bitterness and Resentment

The wounds of betrayal can be easily spotted as they either cause you to bleed out or take you out completely. However, it's the parasites and diseases that can cause our faith to become so infested we end up rubbing away our protective coats against the tree bark of bitterness and resentment. Trying to rub away these irritations instead of allowing God to clean our wounds only leads to more friction from parasites digging into our lives which then leads to the untimely death of our faith.

To be honest, what truly rubbed everyone up the wrong way wasn't the fact that our campus pastor had embezzled funds from our church or from the eight other campuses, although that was bad enough to get our heads around. It was the fact that the church board decided not to press charges against our pastor. These festering wounds of not seeing justice only attracted more flies, and we all know flies can carry diseases, hampering the healing process. If the deep wounds that have come from the arrows of betrayal are compounded by a church culture that either, (1), make excuses for the moral failure or (2), tries to cover it all up, then the consequences of allowing these parasites to infect the wound can be worse than the wound itself.

> **The wounds of betrayal can be easily spotted as they either cause you to bleed out or take you out completely.**

Left half-dead and disappointed

The parable of the good Samaritan is well known. Whether you're a believer or not, the principles within the story are deeply ingrained in each one of us because nobody likes to be ignored or passed by when they are wounded and hurting. The story of the good Samaritan is found in Luke 10:30-36, and it is Jesus' response to a religious scholar who was trying to justify his feelings of guilt. Jesus starts the parable with a Jewish man who had been robbed and left for dead and two religious people see he is wounded but they choose to walk on by.

However, a Samaritan helps the Jewish man thus driving Jesus' point home that we are all to love our neighbour.

But it's verses 33 and 34 that I want to bring your attention to because these two verses help us to understand how important it is for our wounds to be cleaned. '…finally, another man, a Samaritan, came upon the bleeding man and was moved with

Nobody likes to be ignored or passed by when they are wounded and hurting.

tender compassion for him. He stooped down and gave him first aid, pouring olive oil on his wounds, disinfecting them with wine and bandaging them to stop the bleeding.' When a moral failure occurs within the church walls, we demand justice, and if we do not see justice then we feel robbed by the ones we thought would protect and help us. The parasite that got in under the skin of our church was one of wondering whether our campus pastor's response was truly remorseful because he understood what he did was wrong and he was ready to face the consequences of his actions, or could his weeping response be because he had finally been caught in the act?

Infected scabs that form over your wounding that can be caused by parasitic thinking, leaving a messy blood trail behind us, one that the hunter, Satan is all too willing to follow up on. Therefore, we need to allow the cleansing blood of Jesus to disinfect the parasites and diseases that can infect wounds from the deep betrayal so that our faith doesn't die. Counselling and pastoral care helps in the process, but it is the disinfecting power found in the blood of Jesus that is crucial to forgiving the moral failure of someone you held in high regard so that you are cleansed and can move forward.

If you feel like you've been left half-dead and disappointed and your faith has died due to lack of compassion and care because religion chose to walk by you, then I am sorry. The truth is that religion realised that by helping you out it could potentially cost it something.

You needed Someone to be so moved with compassion with the sight of your wounds that they willingly pour their wine into your infected thinking.

You needed Someone to be so moved with compassion with the sight of your wounds that they willingly pour their wine into your infected thinking. The difference between Jesus and religion is that religion asks if you have earned enough credit to receive my help, but Jesus poured out Himself for us on the cross, regardless of whether we deserved the help or not.

To be honest, it took many years for my husband and I to heal from the parasites that infected the wounds left from the betrayal of our pastor, and we had to take the journey that led to complete forgiveness so we could move on. Sadly, my children are still collateral damage from that battle and are still running. Forgiveness only comes when we allow Jesus to pour olive oil into our wounding and disinfect where the parasites and disease got in with His cleansing blood. The cleaning of our wounds didn't cost Jesus something, like the good Samaritan in the parable, it cost Him *everything*.

Endnotes: Chapter Six

Ref 1   Collins, Suzanne. 2012. *The Hunger Games. [1].* London: Scholastic, Cop.

Ref 2   eatingthewild.com/where-to-shoot-an-elk-with-an-arrow/

Ref 3   elk-hunting-tips.net/blood-trailing.html

Ref 4   Psalm 91:4 *The Passion Translation: New Testament with Psalms, Proverbs, and Song of Songs, Second Edition.* Passion & Fire Ministries, Inc. BroadStreet Publishing: 2018.

Ref 5   https://dreamingandsleeping.com/elk-spirit-animal-symbolism-and-meaning/

Ref 6   Hunting.net.com/articles/Elk Anatomy- parasite and diseases.html

CHAPTER SEVEN

Rubbing Antlers

'Jesus desires to heal our wounds. But we often do not let Him heal them because it is not the easiest road to take.' [1]
JOHN BEVERE

Impressing a cow during rutting season so he can mate with her is a bull elk's number one goal and the more attractive his antlers are the better. Polishing them against trees gives the antlers that eye-catching look which no female elk can resist. Plus, the rubbing of antlers is also a way of letting other males know who's the boss as the competition to win over a cow can become quite fierce. The antlers are made up of bone and have a protective covering of leather-like skin which have blood vessels so that oxygen is provided to the antlers for growth. This thin layer of skin is called, velvet, and when the antlers are fully grown the velvet coating falls off. [2] In the same way, we try to impress God and others by polishing our antlers of service and sacrifice until they catch God's attention, believing our try-hard life will indeed impress Him.

Lying in a hospital bed completely still in the emergency department on my husband's forty-second birthday while having a spinal tap procedure performed on me, wasn't exactly what I had planned. At thirty-eight years old, I had hit the wall. The train of thought from the performing life I had been travelling on had finally ran out of track and the crash came suddenly and unexpectantly. The symptoms I had showed were all the signs of meningitis and I just wanted to curl up into a ball and die from the pain in my head. For two weeks I hadn't been able to keep any food down and had to stay in a darkened room for most of the day because the light hurt my eyes, making the agonising pain almost unbearable in my head.

My family were very worried as I showed no signs of getting better and my kids knew something bad was happening to me as they hardly saw me because I was either holed up in my bedroom or laying on the couch trying to at least engage with the family in some small way. My performance-based, saying 'yes' to everything attitude had to go. I was a complete mess. However, I was well loved because the kindness from our church was wonderful. People prepared meals and our friends came to our house to pray over me which helped my family to know that they were not alone in this fight. And as we waited for a

> We try to impress God and others by polishing our antlers of service and sacrifice until they catch God's attention, believing our try-hard life will indeed impress Him.

breakthrough in my condition, the tests for meningitis thankfully came back negative. However, this still left the doctors wondering what was causing my intense pain. Finally, after what felt like a lifetime and numerous trips to the emergency ward, a doctor discovered through more testing, that I had a severe case of sinusitis, which is an infection and inflammation of the sinuses. Once the doctor put me on a course of antibiotics, I started to feel better and eventually, after another four weeks of recovery, I felt well enough and strong enough to go back to work as the pastor's personal assistant.

Shedding Antlers

A bull elk's testosterone level peaks during the breeding season and their magnificent, shiny antlers are on full display to attract females. However, elks are part of the Cervidae family and males shed their antlers each year in spring when their levels of testosterone drop to base level, telling the body to produce osteoclasts which breaks down and reabsorbs bone. Eventually, the antler falls off, leaving a stump called a pedicle that is attached to the elk's skull.[3]

After returning from my lengthy illness, I thanked my friend in the leadership team for covering my role during my time off. That was until my pastor's told me that they had revised the position of personal assistant while I'd been away sick and transferred the paid role to my friend who was now the church bookkeeper. Renaming the role 'bookkeeper' didn't hide the fact that she was doing exactly the same things as I had done as a personal assistant, and everyone knew it. I suddenly grasped that all those coffee dates she'd invited me to had a hidden agenda attached to them. She had played the game of befriending me ever since we had first met, and I remember she said to me once, 'I make sure I do whatever it takes to win'. Clearly, I was the loser in this game. So, my impressive title of personal assistant had been shed like a bull elk's antlers and I was left with the stumps of neglect and disappointment. All my polishing and performing that I believed was impressing my pastor's had only led to burnout, and once again I felt confused and rejected by the very ones who I had called 'friend'.

Polished Distraction

Hunters take advantage of bull elk's raking trees to polish their antlers. With their eyes closed, busily making sure every part of their points are polished and rubbed, plus the noise from the rustling of leaves means the elk cannot see or hear a hunter creeping toward them.[4] All the movement within the trees reveals to the hunter their location, making the bull elk an easy target. Distracted by all his busyness, the bull elk lets his guard down not realising that he has allowed himself to become vulnerable for an arrow or shot that will start a blood trail yet again.

Like the elk, we can become so distracted by all our striving to impress others that we make trouble for ourselves. The hunter, Satan doesn't need to shoot

> We've let our thinking spiral downwards into a bothered and anxious state and our old wounds of abandonment and betrayal start to bleed out again.

another arrow from his quiver to start the blood trail because when we've allowed ourselves to become so distracted by a performance-based mindset, we've let our thinking spiral downwards into a bothered and anxious state and our old wounds of abandonment and betrayal start to bleed out again.

You don't need to get close to see a leader who leads from a performance-based mindset, you can spot them from a distance because the trees in every department within the church are rustling with all their frenzied movement and activity of polishing their antlers. The dysfunctional actions of a try-hard, performance-based, need for approval leader only causes competition between other leaders and all that glint and gloss will lead to old wounds oozing out once again.

The Good Part

Perhaps this is why we are so drawn to the story of Mary and Martha in Luke chapter 10:38-42? The story starts with Martha welcoming Jesus into her home. 'Now while they were on their way, Jesus entered a village [called Bethany], and a woman named Martha welcomed Him into her home. She had a sister named Mary, who seated herself at the Lord's feet, and was continually listening to his teaching. But Martha was very busy and distracted with all her serving responsibilities; and she approached Him and said, 'Lord, is it no concern to You that my sister has left me to do the serving alone? Tell her to help me and do her part.' But the Lord replied to her, 'Martha, Martha, you are worried and bothered and anxious about so many things; but one thing is necessary, for Mary has chosen the good part [that which is to her advantage], which will not be taken away from her.'⁵

I believe we're a little hard on Martha when we read this story because it's so easy to point fingers at people who feel they need to perform. However, hosting Jesus and his disciples would have involved a lot of work for Martha and seeing her sister doing nothing but listening to Jesus' teaching would have irritated even the most willing of servants. And yet, knowing how much work would be involved, Martha still *welcomed Jesus*. She still opened her home because hospitality was probably the only way she knew how to show devotion to Jesus. Sometimes serving others is the only way some people know how to show their adoration toward Jesus, and that's okay. But the danger is that because they're so busy rustling trees in every department of the church trying to get those antlers gleaming so their reputation of a servant is upheld, they become distracted by all the *doing for* Jesus instead of making sure they are *being with* Jesus first.

> **They become distracted by all the *doing for* Jesus instead of making sure they are *being with* Jesus first.**

The good part about the story which Jesus was pointing to is the fact He knew both sister's hearts and He didn't dismiss the need for Martha's serving responsibilities. We all have a responsibility in the church to serve each other. Nevertheless, I don't think this story is really about serving at all because if you peel back the layers, I believe, Jesus was showing His male disciples the importance of women becoming disciples in a culture that only saw the role of a women as a homemaker.⁶ If we look at the bigger picture, we understand that most people sat on chairs or reclined on couches at festivities when this story took place. But disciples sat at the feet of their teachers and discipleship was not permitted if you were a woman. Mary was breaking protocol sitting at the feet of Jesus and this behaviour could have perhaps offended Jesus' disciples,[6] so Jesus was possibly bringing this to everyone's attention by saying to Martha, 'you are worried and bothered and anxious about so many things; but one thing is necessary, for Mary has chosen the good part'. Jesus was saying that being His disciple was the most important thing to do and Mary's posture, her keenness, her hunger, even though she was a woman, even though her role was seen as homemaker by her culture, was to sit at Jesus' feet and learn from Him.

Posture

The posture of a bull elk when he's polishing his antlers is one of distraction. His whole focus is to shine up his antlers to impress. But the posture of Mary wasn't about what people expected of her. She wasn't worried about what people thought she should or shouldn't do. Her responsibility, her calling was to become a disciple of Jesus and if that meant disappointing her sister and rubbing her up the wrong way, then so be it. My imagination runs wild as I think more and more about this story. I'd like to believe that Mary was possibly helping her sister serve the guests before Jesus arrived. It could be that she was handing out a tray of pre-dinner nibbles and was just about to head back into the kitchen when Jesus showed up and started teaching His disciples something of importance. And as Mary moved around the crowd with her half empty tray of finger foods, she perhaps thought to herself, 'How did I end up doing this?' because she suddenly felt hungry. Not a hunger for food but a hunger to hear more of Jesus' teaching. Mary would have understood her posture of sitting at the feet of Jesus would have shocked the Jewish men in her presence, but she pushed through those feelings and did it anyway.

When you are called to do something, you need to decide what needs to stay in your life and what needs to change. Posture is important when Jesus shows up and we need to learn to sit at His feet. Just like my little imaginary story about Mary, you need to ask yourself the question, 'How did I end up doing this?'. My burnout came from a faulty mindset that I had to do everything because I believed it was what was expected of me. I do recall my pastor once commenting on my busyness and he said, 'Don't sacrifice your family on the altar of ministry.' Wise words if you actually stop and listen to them, which of course, I didn't. Leaders can become so malnourished from not feeding on the Word and sitting at Jesus' feet that they become weak, and weakness is what the hunter, Satan looks for. No predator takes on the strongest in the herd, he only picks off the fragile and feeble elks that have exhausted themselves from polishing their antlers too much.

Respectable try-hard, people-pleasing, performance-based leaders will never ever check their posture. Good posture

> **No predator takes on the strongest in the herd, he only picks off the fragile and feeble elks that have exhausted themselves from polishing their antlers too much.**

requires listening to your body otherwise it leads to loss of strength, and this is why the hunter, Satan doesn't need to shoot another arrow. The disappointment we feel from all our expectations not being met can bring back the trauma of our past wounding causing us to bleed out which saps our strength. We wonder where Jesus is when it all goes wrong, as we feel the sting of the wounds of abandonment once again. Our question changes from 'How did I end up doing this?' to 'How could you let this happen, Jesus?'. Burned out and burnt by the church because you've given it your all. No more shaking of trees from all your polishing activity, only the shaky ground you're now standing on because you've lost your footing, beating yourself up because you allowed yourself to get distracted which has given the hunter, Satan access to your blood trail again.

> We wonder where Jesus is when it all goes wrong, as we feel the sting of the wounds of abandonment once again.

Unstable Ground

When you feel discarded and dumped the first thing you want to know is why. And sadly, weak leadership will skirt around the reason behind their decisions instead of being direct. If the reason for a decision is not made clear, we then struggle with the process of why that choice was made. When you're on the unstable ground of an unresolved issue it changes your perspective on who to trust causing you to lose your confidence in who God called you to be. So, you run away and hide, wondering if God is really for you. You want to know if you are valued, you want your leaders to show you how much you are worth because those thoughts that are spinning out of control in your head, trapping you in a cycle of distraction is not a good place to be. This is why performance-based, try-hard serving is so dangerous. We are so busy polishing our antlers that we become distracted and lose our focus on choosing the good part.

> **Like Mary, choose the good part.**

Dear friend, perhaps you have felt, or you are experiencing right now the sting of rejection from pastors because of an unresolved issue. You've asked questions but still, you cannot seem to get to the 'why' of the reason the decision was made. And now you're hiding because you are worried and bothered and anxious about so many things. Like Mary, choose the good part. Choose to sit at the feet of Jesus and allow Him to take care of your wounds.

All Wrapped Up

If you're led to believe that your identity, value, and worth are all wrapped up in how well you serve and perform within a church, then you need to change your posture. I have learned the hard way and when I start to feel myself picking at the scars of leading from a performance-based mindset, I think of Jesus. If He bowed down to everyone's expectations, then He would have never sacrificed Himself and died on a cross. Jesus was always disappointing people. He faithfully lived out the purpose He was born to do and served people while doing it. However, He never became burned out because He always came back to a posture of listening to what His Father was teaching Him. When you balance serving with posturing, other people's expectations will not feel so demanding. More importantly, you stop being afraid of saying that little word, 'no' so you stay healthy. Our self-worth isn't found in how much we are doing for God, it's in our relationship with Him. Stanley Grenz puts it so simply when he said, 'We scrutinize how others treat us and seek to determine what they think of us. In the end, however, our value is not based on how others perceive our worth. Ultimately, only God's opinion of us matters.'[7]

> Our self-worth isn't found in how much we are doing for God, it's in our relationship with Him.

Child and Father can so easily become slave and master when we serve from a performance-based mindset. Now I can see that God, in His kindness, stripped that position of personal assistant away from me because I had put my identity in my job instead of in Him. I had scrutinised the actions of my pastors and my friend on how badly they had treated me and wrapped up my self-worth in their opinions of me. At the time my wound of abandonment bled out for a few months because I was angry with my pastors and my friend. I felt like a fool because I had been duped again. How could I be so naïve? Like Martha, I had been pulled away though all my busyness and I believed that Jesus didn't care about me. But over time, I realised it was for my own good and the good of my family. Jesus needs to take some things away from us. It's tough and it's hard and it feels unfair, but Jesus is into the long game, not the 100-metre sprint where you'll burn out too quickly. I believe I wouldn't be doing what I'm doing now if I stayed in that role at that church. God's Kingdom requires us to live an all-in life. But Jesus also reminds us of the dangers of being rubbed the wrong way by choosing to impress God with a try-hard life. 'Are you weary, carrying a heavy burden? Then come to me. I will refresh your life, for I am your oasis. Simply join your life with mine. Learn my ways and you'll discover that I'm gentle, humble, easy to please. You will find refreshment and rest in me. For all that I require of you will be pleasant and easy to bear.'[8] (Matthew 11:28-30)

Endnotes: Chapter Seven

Ref 1   Bevere, John. *The Bait Of Satan: Living Free From The Deadly Trap Of Offense.* 2004. Charisma House, Lake Mary, Florida.

Ref 2   animalqueries.com/what-are-antlers-made-of/

Ref 3   krebscreek.com/why-when-and-where-do-bull-elk-lose-their-antlers/

Ref 4   suwanneeriverranch.com/ElkRubbingTrees.htm

Ref 5   Luke 10:38-42 *Amplified Holy Bible: Captures the Full Meaning behind the Original Greek and Hebrew.* 2015. Grand Rapids, Michigan: Zondervan.

Ref 6   Keener, Craig S. 1993. *The IVP Bible Background Commentary: New Testament.* Downers Grove, Ill. InterVarsity Press.

Ref 7   Grenz, Stanley, J, and Jay T. Smith. 2015. *Created for Community: Connecting Christian Belief with Christian Living.* Grand Rapids, Mi: Baker Academic.

Ref 8   Matthew 11:28-30. *The Passion Translation: New Testament with Psalms, Proverbs, and Song of Songs, Second Edition.* Passion & Fire Ministries, Inc. BroadStreet Publishing: 2018.

CHAPTER EIGHT

Bugle Call

'Bitterness has no friends. There is no container known to man that will hold it. It always leaks out onto those we love the most.' [1]
KRIS VALLOTTON

In chapter 3, we learnt that a hunter mimics the bugle calls of an elk so he can lure it away from the herd. So too, a wounded believer can 'bugle call' their bitterness and cynicism to other believers while still mimicking and going through the motions of church life.

I found I was bugle calling my bitterness onto my husband from being let go from my personal assistant job in the church. At the time, I didn't realise how much of a toll my lengthy illness had affected my mental health. Even though I was functioning as normal on the surface, the trauma from my wounds was showing up in my 'bugling' at my husband. The whole ordeal had left its mark and the circle of questions of 'How could this happen to me, God?' to 'What is my purpose now, God?' infected my prayer times as I picked at my wounds of rejection and abandonment. The hunter, Satan had rendered my view of the leadership as people who cannot be fully trusted which caused my faith to become defective. Allowing the wounds of betrayal, abandonment, and rejection to become infected meant I was doing the hunter's work for him. Bugle calling all my bitterness and criticism meant that there was no need for the hunter to shoot another arrow…well, not just yet…not before I felt secure and brave enough to came out from my hiding place.

> **Allowing the wounds of betrayal, abandonment, and rejection to become infected meant I was doing the hunter's work for him.**

For The Next Stage Of The Journey

After letting me go in the position of their personal assistant, my pastors arranged a meeting with myself and my husband as they wanted to chat to us about something. Like a wounded, wild elk, I was cautious at first to let my guard down and wondered what they were going to say. The pastors knew our hearts were still to see the church flourish and asked us if we would consider co-leading the church plant our own church had birthed some months earlier. The leader who had taken over my role gifted me with a journal with a handwritten inscription of, 'for the next stage of the journey'. I had to supress the thoughts that it was her parting gift that made sure my departure was sealed and I was truly out of the way. Regardless of my thoughts on her motivation of her gift, little did I know then that the next phase in my journey would require all the strength and stamina I could muster.

The church plant was an hour's drive away from where we lived, so a two hour round trip each Sunday morning meant we would have to juggle our family commitments and arrange for our children to be picked up and dropped off by our friends at our own church as our son was still part of the worship team. After chatting it over we knew it would be a stretch, not only for ourselves but also our children, however, we were sure this was the right direction God was leading us. I remember my close friend sharing some of her concerns with me about accepting this role of co-leading the church plant. Preaching, pastoral care and everything else that was needed to gain momentum to build the church plant from the ground up would be a huge undertaking and she reminded me that I had already suffered from complete burnout. Plus, it was a volunteer role and not a staff position. Regardless, I decided to dismiss my friend's concerns because before chatting with her, I had already made up my mind. I was going because my pastors needed me to help out and I was excited about co-leading the church plant with my husband. But to be honest, my friend's concerns were valid and if I had had been really truthful with her and myself, I would have said that I felt pressured to go. I felt that if I had of said no, then I wouldn't be walking on the path God wanted me to be on. If I'd have been authentic, I would have let her know that if I didn't go, in some way, I felt I was being disobedient, and I didn't want to be out of God's will by not accepting the call.

The Arrow Came Swiftly

Things were going well, but we were only a few months into our leadership roles and our kids were already starting to feel neglected. As a family it felt as though we were living separate lives and the toll of all the travelling, not only on a Sunday but during the week too, was telling on us and our car's odometer! My husband was still working shifts and he would often be found setting up all the technical stuff to run the Sunday service straight off the back of a twelve-hour night shift. As we got to know the couple, we were co-leading with more and more, we felt a sense that they were nervous of getting out into the community. We communicated with our pastors that we were looking at a new building to run the church from, somewhere more central in the town. Our pastors were supportive and happy we were so committed to seeing the church flourish.

However, it became obvious that the woman of the couple who helped co-lead with us didn't like me to think or question her on how we were going to move the church forward. The arrow from the hunter's bow that was shot one Sunday morning just before we were about to start the service came swiftly. It landed right into the scar tissue from my previous wounding and as the wound bled out quickly from her controlling behaviour, I felt completely humiliated. I don't know how I managed to get through to the end of the service, but I knew that the hunter, Satan was silencing my 'voice' in ministry again. Undoubtedly, this woman liked to be in control, and she had used every bit of her authoritative power to make sure I received that message loud and clear.

Turning The Tables

A savvy, smart hunter understands the difference between *the* rut and *a* rut so he can change his bugle calling strategy accordingly. The rut is the season when breeding starts to occur, however, a rut is when it is actually taking place. With this knowledge the hunter can now create a false scenario. Instead of his old bugling strategy of finding a bull that is wanting to fight another bull to claim the 'hot' cow, the hunter just needs to make sure the excited bull is within ear shot of the fake sounds he is bugling that mimic another bull with a cow who has come into oestrus. Now armed with this effective strategy, the hunter has 'reversed the tables'[2] on the elk who will not see the hunter's arrow coming until it's too late.

Honestly, I did not see this arrow coming. Satan had turned the tables on me this time. Clearly his position was of a disadvantage, so he needed to change his strategy. My frustration turned into discouragement which eventually turned into sadness. After all the other arrows and bullets that the hunter had fired at me over the years, I felt that I couldn't recover from this one. This arrow was the deadliest of them all because it had ripped through and damaged my trust in God. I was bone tired, and I was lost. Tired of being in leadership, tired of continuously serving, tired of volunteering, tired of Church. Period. Feeling misplaced and adrift I was done with it all. I couldn't go back, and I couldn't move forward. We'd failed in the church plant because it was now abundantly clear that we had taken on a responsibility that was never ours to shoulder.

Tracking And Recovering Wounded Souls

It's important for a hunter to track down and recover an elk he started a blood trail with, otherwise all the hard work it took to search for the animal feels like a lost cause. The decomposed carcass of a poor, wounded elk means that an unfortunate hunter was unable to track and recover it in time.[3] Perhaps this is how you feel right now dear friend? Your faith feels like it's been left to perish because nobody tracked you down and recovered you? You wouldn't care even if the hunter, Satan found you, you'd welcome that final shot that would take you out completely so that God, your faith, and the Church were just a distant memory. Terrible wounding can numb us to the point where we let these thoughts swirl in our heads.

> **No matter how long you've run or how wounded you are, Jesus will find you.** He searches into the deepest, darkest holes where your wounded soul is mired with muck and clay.

And yet, if you've sat with me up until this moment in this little wooden cabin in the forest while you are warming yourself by the fire, listening to me sharing my story so far, you'll wonder how my belief in God survived. You'll look at my scars and be curious as to how I was rescued from that dark moment in my faith. But like I said before, no matter how long you've run or how wounded you are, Jesus will find you. He searches into the deepest, darkest holes where your wounded soul is mired with muck and clay. Jesus listens for the weakened whispers of the desperate and lonely. And with a gentle hand, He pulls you out of that place, dries your tears and holds you until you're steady enough to continue the journey again.[4]

The Disinfectant of His Truth

Jesus found me hidden in that dark place and poured His Word of healing onto my wounding. It was a scripture I shared with you in the introduction of this book, taken from Isaiah 58, '… If you take away the yoke from your midst, The pointing of the finger, and speaking wickedness, If you extend your soul to the hungry And satisfy the afflicted soul, Then your light shall dawn in the darkness, And your darkness shall be as the noonday. The LORD will guide you continually And satisfy your soul in drought And strengthen your bones; You shall be like a watered garden, And like a spring of water, whose waters do not fail. Those from among you Shall build the old waste places; You shall raise up the foundations of many generations; And you shall be called the Repairer of the Breach, the Restorer of Streets to Dwell In.'

> **Jesus found me hidden in that dark place and poured His Word of healing onto my wounding.**

As we know, disinfecting any wound stings, and this cleansing passage hurt – a lot! When we're wounded and Jesus recovers us so the hunter, Satan doesn't finish us off, the last thing we want is more pain inflicted on us. We want nice, fluffy Bible passages from Jesus that sooth our brow and rub our backs, saying, 'There, there child, you have every right to sound out your bugle call of bitterness. You are truly justified to point that finger toward those whose fault it was that something you tried to carry has failed. Bugle away and let everyone know that you were wronged by the people you regarded as family.' However, God doesn't work like that. He knows that the short-term discomfort from the disinfecting truth of His Word is going to be far better for you in the long run than patching up those swollen, festering wounds with Band-Aid, soundbite theology that just covers the problem over instead of dealing with it.

Surrogate Dreams

'You need to go back' was the sentence I was pretending I hadn't heard in my spirit as I was still wondering why God had administered that painful scripture from Isaiah chapter 58 into my wounding. In amongst all my thoughts of wanting to quit church and run away like I had done in my past, I decided to watch one of my favourite speakers, an English lead pastor of life church UK, named, Charlotte Gambill. I've always liked her preaching style and maybe it's because she's English like myself could possibly, perhaps, have something to do with it! As I started to scroll through her sermons on YouTube, I spotted a title called, 'Girl on the run'.[6] I smiled to myself. God had got this little wounded, runaway elk cornered.

> **I smiled to myself. God had got this little wounded, runaway elk cornered.**

She read the story of Hagar in Genesis 16 and one of the points she made was 'a surrogate for someone else's dream'. Charlotte went on to say that 'we cannot fulfill our dream through someone else.' [6] In other words, we can't birth our dreams through someone else. It has to be God. Wow. It was like a truth ointment soaking into my wounding. Now I understood that even though we so desperately wanted to help see the church plant flourish, it had been our old pastor's dream. I remember our new pastor mentioned that he felt that the church plant was like a baby in an incubator, and it needed care and nurturing. It all seemed very noble and sacrificial to take on this 'baby'. As leaders, we were willing to take custody and guardianship of the church plant and I believe this is why we felt as though we'd failed. However, God was showing me that we hadn't failed because it was never our dream to begin with, and clearly, it wasn't part of God's plan for what He had called us to do. Just like Hagar I had a 'a runaway spirit'[6] and was carrying a surrogate 'baby' for someone else who couldn't birth their own dream because of their moral failure. Truth be told, I knew I had become pregnant with something that caused me to love preaching God's Word while helping the church plant, and this pregnancy of ministry had ruffled a few feathers with 'Sarai'. The two women leaders who had caused me to run further and further away from my calling went by different names, however, the sting in the wounding of the story of Hagar running away was the same as mine because God had asked her to go back too.

'Where Are You Planning to Go?'

'Abram (to Sarai): 'Sarai – look, she's still your servant girl. Do whatever you want with her. She's under your control.' So, Sarai clamped down on Hagar severely, and Hagar ran away. The Special Messenger of the Eternal One found Hagar alone by a spring of water out in the desert. It was the spring of water along the road that went to Shur. Special Messenger: 'Hagar, Sarai's servant girl? Where have you come from, and where are you planning to go?'

Hagar: 'I am running away from my mistress, Sarai!' Special Messenger: 'Hagar, go back to your mistress, and change your attitude. Be respectful and listen to her instructions. You're pregnant, and you need to go home. Trust me: I am going to give you many children and many descendants, so many you won't be able to count them!' (Genesis 16:6-10)[7]

God was asking me the same questions, 'Where have you come from?' My answer, 'from a place where I had become a surrogate mother to a baby church.' 'Where are you planning to go?' My answer, 'I am running away from two leaders. The first pilfered my job from me and the second humiliated and belittled me in front of people in a Sunday service.' God's answer to my response, 'You need to go back.' Ouch. 'You need to change your attitude.' Ouch. 'You need to listen to instructions.' Ouch, ouch, ouch.

The disinfectant of Isaiah chapter 58 stung. '...take away the yoke from your midst...the pointing of the finger...speaking wickedness.' Ugh! God was asking me to extend my soul to the hungry and satisfy the afflicted soul. What about *my* malnourishment, God? What about *my* afflicted soul? Leadership

> What about *my* malnourishment, God? What about *my* afflicted soul?

can be so unfair sometimes, but the good news was that there was a promise attached to my willingness to surrender. 'The LORD will guide you continually And satisfy your soul in drought And strengthen your bones; You shall be like a watered garden, And like a spring of water, whose waters do not fail. Those from among you shall build the old waste places; You shall raise up the foundations of many generations; And you shall be called the Repairer of the Breach, the Restorer of Streets to Dwell In.'

> The only way forward was to walk in forgiveness if I was to stop my wounds from bleeding out.

As hard as it was, I knew God had called us back to our church for a reason. To satisfy our souls and strengthen our bones. So, I decided to return back to our church because the only way forward was to walk in forgiveness if I was to stop my wounds from bleeding out.

Endnotes: Chapter Eight.

Ref 1   Vallotton, Kris, and Bill Johnson. 2017. *The Supernatural Ways of Royalty :Discovering your Rights and Privileges of Being a Son or Daughter of God.* Shippensburg, Pa: Destiny Images Publishers.

Ref 2   elkbros.com/hunting-the-elk-rut-what-does-that-really-mean/

Ref 3   realtree.com/big-game-hunting/articles/how-to-recover-a-wounded-elk

Ref 4   Psalm 40:1-4. Ecclesia Bible Society. 2012. *The Voice Bible: Step into the Story of Scripture.* Nashville: Thomas Nelson.

Ref 5   Isaiah 58:9-12. *Spiritual Warfare Bible.* 2012. Lake Mary, Florida, Charisma House

Ref 6   Charlotte Gambill 'Girl on the run' sermon YouTube.2015.

Ref 7   Genesis 16:6-10. Ecclesia Bible Society. 2012. *The Voice Bible: Step into the Story of Scripture.* Nashville: Thomas Nelson.

CHAPTER NINE

Close-Range Shots

> *'Solomon tells us that the ways of wisdom,*
> *- that is, Christ - 'are ways of pleasantness'.*
> *But how so, when some of them are ways of suffering?'* [1]
> WILLIAM GURNALL

In order to get a close-range shot, hunters use a decoy cardboard elk – a dummy elk – to lure the bull elk into believing he has found a 'hot' female elk to mate with. If the excited elk falls for this tactic, then it's game over. There are many strategies to trick an elk as they are intelligent, adaptable animals that are quick learners, so a hunter needs to continuously keep coming up with calculated, tactical moves when hunting elk. Decoys are used to deceive and cheat a bull elk by directing all his efforts into attracting a fake, cardboard female elk instead of using all his energy into pursuing a legitimate female elk. When the bull elk realises that he is never going to win over the decoy, dummy elk with his performance-based display, his excitement turns to fear as he feels the sting of the arrow from the hunter's bow pierce his skin. Likewise, the hunter, Satan's tactics are just as savvy when it comes to extinguishing our excitement in our faith. Every diversion from his decoys directs all our energy and effort toward something that is fake rather than real and the arrow aimed at us is designed to take us out of our mission, our purpose, and our calling.

> **The hunter, Satan's tactics are just as savvy when it comes to extinguishing our excitement in our faith.**

With a changed attitude, the return to our church was welcomed by our pastors. We decided to try another campus in the movement which was still under the leadership of our pastors rather than go back to our original campus as we felt this was a necessary move so our wounds could continue to heal from everything we had been through. Our pastors kindly gave us team leader roles even though I felt we had failed them in the church plant. This transition was welcomed by the leadership team at the campus as we knew some of the leaders already.

About a year later, the associate pastor and my good friend from the other church campus asked if I would like to attend a two-day conference with them that was aimed specifically for women preachers on how to effectively use their voice. My friends had clearly noticed how 'pregnant' I had become with what God was calling me to do and so of course I agreed to go as this would be a good opportunity. A few weeks before we attended the conference, God gave me another scripture. It was still in Isaiah, however, this time it felt like a call to arms rather than a stinging disinfect for my wounds. It was about the consequences of complacency.

> 'Rise up you women who are at ease,
> hear my voice; you complacent daughters,
> give ear to my speech.
> In a year and some days,
> you will be troubled, you complacent women;
> for the vintage will fail,
> the gathering will not come.
> Tremble you women who are at ease;
> be troubled, you complacent ones;
> strip yourselves, make yourselves bare,
> and gird sackcloth on your waists.
> People shall mourn upon their breasts
> For the pleasant fields, for the fruitful vine.
> On the land of my people will come up thorns and briers,
> Yes, on all the happy homes in the joyous city;
> Because the palaces will be forsaken,
> The bustling city will be deserted.
> The forts and towers will become lairs forever,
> A joy of wild donkeys, a pasture of flocks –
> Until the Spirit is poured upon us from on high,
> And the wilderness becomes a fruitful field,
> And the fruitful field is counted as a forest.
> Isaiah 32: 9-15 (NKJV)

As I headed to the conference, I wrote this scripture in the front page of my notebook. I wrote two sentences in red ink rather than blue ink that stood out to me, 'the gathering will not come' and 'until the Spirit is poured upon us from on high'. Even though I had kept running away from my calling for years, kept hiding, kept being continually wounded by the hunter, Satan, God had found me, and I knew He was calling me toward something that was good, something that He needed me to not become complacent about, else the gathering will not come. As I felt the stirring by positioning and posturing myself at the women's conference, I wanted the Spirit to pour down from on high so that I could finally birth what had been growing on the inside of me for years which was to preach God's Word whatever way that looked like. In the last session, the speaker invited all the attendees to leave their seats and come down the front if they wanted to receive a fresh word from God for their lives. Many women came forward and the Holy Spirit's presence was tangibly felt within the small church hall where the conference was being held. I felt the nudge from God to leave my seat, so I got up and walked to the front and stood in the line. It had become quite warm in the room, and I had taken off the dark jacket I had been wearing which revealed my sparkly t-shirt emblazoned with a tiger face that had previously been hidden.

    The speaker moved slowly along the line as she spoke the whisperings of Heaven into every woman's hungry heart. Then it was my turn. She looked at me intently and said into her microphone, 'It isn't a coincidence that you decided to wear that t-shirt'. I suddenly had a thought, 'Oh God, now every woman in

> Even though I had kept running away from my calling for years, kept hiding, kept being continually wounded by the hunter, Satan, God had found me.

the room is going to think I wore this tiger face, sparkly t-shirt on purpose!' The speaker continued. 'God is saying that you need to stop meowing like a pussycat and start roaring like a tiger.' Pausing, she said, 'I think you know exactly what I'm talking about.' And there it was, the call to stop meowing, to stop apologising for who I was, to stop being small and shrinking back out of fear, to quit neglecting my gifts to preach and to write and to embrace the leader whom God said I was. After all the running I had found myself again. Correction, God had found me, and He was encouraging me to roar, letting every 'Sarai' that had caused me to run away and hide that I was going to give birth to what was growing on the inside of me whether they liked it or not.

> And there it was, the call to stop meowing, to stop apologising for who I was, to stop being small and shrinking back out of fear.

ROAR!

In the couple of years that followed, I started researching on how to start a blog and I was asked to preach occasionally at our church campus. I even wrote, produced, and directed a three act Christmas play that involved a cast, stage crew, and creative tech team and we performed 'The Christmas Express' stage play over one weekend. But despite all this 'roaring' I still felt I wasn't enough, still felt I had to do everything right in my role at church in case I lost my position to another leader as I had done before. All my fears only fuelled my performance-based mindset, and it was causing tension in my marriage because my husband refused to stand by and watch me get burnout again. I knew he was drawing away from the church more and more and I didn't know how to fix the problem.

Slowly over time, I realised that some of the friends I thought were real were turning out to be fake. Admittedly, I did have a couple of close friends whom I knew genuinely were concerned for me and I was glad of their friendship, and I still am, but like the bull elk, I realised that I was spending all my energy on my performance-based display, burning myself out trying to win the approval of people who were just cardboard cut outs of the leaders I thought they were. I'd fallen for the decoys that the hunter, Satan had set up and now I was entangled in a leadership that was hypnotized by performance rather than servanthood. I prayed about what I should be doing, and the familiar voice of God whispered to me, 'You're looking at the wrong platform.' I didn't understand. I had obeyed His direction to go back to the people I had run away from after the church plant fail, I had changed my attitude, I'd stopped meowing like a pussycat and I was now roaring like a tiger, and now, I was looking at the wrong platform!

Was God warning me that I was in danger of the hunter, Satan pulling back his bow ready for another close-range shot to wound me again? I had fallen for the decoys the hunter had set up because he knew that my performance-based mindset was just covering up my shame and I didn't know how to stop my display toward the decoys. I so desperately wanted to feel needed even though I knew my cardboard cut-out friends were not the real deal.

'Once everyone understands their value, we stop hustling for worthiness and lean into our gifts' [3] Brené Brown reminds every person who seeks validation from fake, cardboard people because it's the sense of value we long for. This is why we push all our energy and effort toward hustling with the decoys because we're looking for real, authentic people to do life with. Once again, God's authentic voice, His real bugle call, was sounding out and I needed to pay attention to it.

Blood Trail of Brokenness

The hunter, Satan knows he can entrap us by following the blood trail of brokenness flowing out from our wounding as we carry our past hurts from church to church, place to place and never really deal with our wounds because we don't notice how much we need healing from our past. Past hurts can cause us to develop a performance-based mindset as we hustle for our worth which only puts a lid on our calling because we wouldn't dare show our authentic, genuine selves just in case our genuineness sets us up to get hurt again. So, we focus all our energy on our performance-based displays, trying desperately to win over the decoy, dummy elks that are never going to be impressed by our performances.

> **Past hurts can cause us to develop a performance-based mindset as we hustle for our worth.**

Wounds make us hide our true selves, and if we don't allow Jesus to deal with them properly then we can't live out an authentic life and have the confidence to lean into our giftings, and so we fall for the decoys the hunter, Satan sets up every time. Something happened in our past experiences to cause us to keep looking for our value and worth in paper-thin people instead of a genuine God. Jesus knows how wounds can limit us, keeping us small and cramped in our hiding so we focus on performing for the decoys instead of cultivating a genuine relationship with Him.

In the Apostle Paul's letter to the Philippians, he calls for followers of Christ to be a community, to love each other and be deep-spirited friends.[4] Performance-based mindsets only creates rivalry and comparison within leadership, instead of an authentic, genuine servanthood mindset that gives space to lead out of the relationship we have with Jesus rather than from our past wounding. We can all fall for the trap of decoy elks because the hunter makes them look so authentic, so real. But a performance-based mindset is relying on people instead of God and He will reveal every illusion, every decoy, every papery thin set up the hunter, Satan uses so you rely on a genuine, authentic relationship with Him. The only approval you need is God's, and He has called you for a purpose. However, you are so malnourished dear, wounded elk, and if you're going to continue along this journey of healing from your wounds, then you're going to need to gain some strength and stamina.

> **We can all fall for the trap of decoy elks because the hunter makes them look so authentic, so real.**

Endnotes: Chapter Nine

Ref 1   Gurnall, William. 2010. *The Christian in Complete Armour*. Peabody, Mass.: Hendrickson ; Edinburgh.

Ref 2   Isaiah 9-15 *Spiritual Warfare Bible*. 2012. Lake Mary, Florida, Charisma House

Ref 3   Brown, Brené. 2018. *Dare to Lead: Brave Work, Tough Conversations, Whole Hearts.* New York Random House.

Ref 4   Philippians 2:1-4. Peterson, Eugene H. 2000. *The Message Bible:* Colorado Springs, Colorado. Navpress.

CHAPTER TEN

Strength and Stamina

'I won't give up on you; I won't leave you. Strength! Courage!' [1]
JOSHUA 1:5

Elks are able to run long distances and need plenty of strength and stamina if they are to outrun predators. This powerful, big game animal is why hunter's desire elk heads to be mounted on their walls, showing how they gained victory over this majestic animal's physical and mental compacity to outrun and outsmart him. To win a prized elk, hunters need to keep changing up their strategy and tactics. What worked last season may not work in the next season, so a successful hunting trip is all in the preparation because no hunter wants to go home empty handed.

Unlike human hunters, Satan has used the same strategies and tactics for a millennium to deplete every ounce of strength and stamina believers need to keep leading the way and help point people to Jesus. If he can bag the ultimate prize which is to mount a leader's head on his already heavily decorated trophy wall, then it's only a matter of time before the herd disperse and go their separate ways. If leaders don't deal with their past wounds then they will be blood trailed by the hunter until all their strength and stamina to outrun him is gone.

> Unlike human hunters, Satan has used the same strategies and tactics for a millennium

After God's warning that Satan was getting ready for a close-range shot because I was caught up in a performance-based leadership team which caused me to look at the wrong platform, my pastors invited our church to attend a healing and deliverance night at another campus within the movement. I decided I needed to attend because I knew I needed healing from my wounding. My strength and stamina were almost consumed because I was so tired of running, so exhausted from being blood trailed by the hunter, Satan, and I certainly didn't want to end up with my head mounted on his trophy wall.

Cleaning the Wounds

After preaching, the healing and deliverance minister asked if anyone needed prayer. Along with many others, I stood in line and surrendered to any cleaning up of my wounds which God needed to do so that my blood trail would dry up, and the hunter couldn't shoot at me anymore. As the minister asked me what I needed prayer for, I found myself saying to him that I didn't feel worthy or good enough. A sentence that was packed full of every wound I'd ever felt. As he started to pray for me, he told me that

I had the spirit of death over me. This was not from birth, but right back when I was first conceived in my mother's womb. This spirit of death had followed me all my life and he commanded it to come out

> I didn't feel worthy or good enough.

and leave me alone. As he prayed for the spirit of death to leave me, I felt the Holy Spirit's power knock me backwards as I collapsed on the floor, weeping uncontrollably in a foetal position for what felt like hours. I felt every wound the hunter, Satan had inflicted on me over many years, was being healed and cleaned by God in those moments. I understand this doesn't happen to everyone. I am all for professional counselling and sometimes it is needed to help process our wounding. But the truth is, whether wounds are healed in moments, or we have to go through a lengthy process, one thing is for sure, we have to stop running long enough so Jesus can clean up our wounds.

Poisonous Thinking

The thing about blood trailing is if you stop running long enough you can look at your wounds and figure out where the hunter, Satan keeps shooting his bullets or arrows. For me, it was always the same arrows of rejection, humiliation, and fear, leading me to the poisonous thinking of believing I would be abandoned again which resulted in my performance-based mindset. Over and over again the hunter, Satan would shoot the same arrows in the same areas. Time and time again he used the same strategies and tactics that worked from one season to the next in my faith. Thankfully, Jesus, in His mercy and goodness delivered me from all my wounding and showed me where my blood trail had begun. Now I needed to find the courage and gain enough strength and stamina to take the next step and to stop focusing on all my past mistakes and failures and see who I was becoming. I needed to stop looking back over my shoulder and step into the future God had for me. In truth, I needed to stop depending on my own strength and lean on God's.

What about you dear friend? Do you need to stop running so you can figure out where the hunter, Satan keeps wounding you? I can guarantee that if you trace your blood trail back far enough, you'll discover a similar theme to your wounding. Once you stop running, you'll suddenly realise how dehydrated and malnourished you are. All that running away from God has left you hungry and you need some provision to build up your strength and stamina.

Do you need to stop running so you can figure out where the hunter, Satan keeps wounding you?

God wants to supernaturally infuse you with strength, so you stand victorious with the force of his explosive power flowing in and through you. ² But this requires you to stop looking back at all your past mistakes and failures.

If I'm Completely Honest with You...

Exodus chapter 16 is where we read about the Israelites walking toward the desert of sin.

They were only about two months into their journey toward the Promised Land after leaving Egypt. However, they made the mistake of looking back. 'It would be better if we had died by the hand of the Eternal in Egypt. At least we had plenty to eat and drink, for our pots were stuffed with meat and we had as much bread as we wanted. But now you have brought the entire community out to the desert to starve us to death.' [3] God heard their complaint and sent provision to rain down on the Israelites. 'Look! I will cause bread to rain down from heaven for you, and the people will go out and gather a helping of it each day. I will test them to see if they are willing to live by My instructions.'[4]

I don't know about you, but I can see that some of my wounds were unable to heal properly because I wouldn't allow myself to completely rely on God. The shame which attaches itself to wounds from the past can sometimes be harder to heal from than the wound itself. Once you start to pick at the scab it oozes out quickly, and if I'm completely honest with you, I still have moments of feeling along my scabby scars of shame, picking at them because I'm afraid to let God take full control of my life because of my deep fear of being humiliated again. I know, it's hard to fathom that someone who is writing about their wounds turning into valuable scars can still encounter feelings of shame from time to time. But, if I'm guiding you through the process of healing from your wounds and pain which will lead you to your greatest calling, we need to sit here in this moment together. Brené Brown says that 'Scars are easier to talk about than they are to show, with all the remembered feelings laid bare.'[5] Like the

> **The shame which attaches itself to wounds from the past can sometimes be harder to heal from than the wound itself.**

Israelites we would rather return back to the controlled slavery of Egypt because it sure beats starving to death in the desert where we have to face our fears. But God rescued and redeemed us from slavery, and we need to keep walking in the freedom Jesus died for. If we keep depending on ourselves to find the strength and stamina to keep moving toward the Promised Land, then God will keep us in the desert for as long as it takes until we surrender to His instructions and rely totally on Him.

The Messy Middle Part

We never want to hear about the messy middle part of a redemption story, however, the Jesus I know wouldn't want a cleaned and sterilized version of our testimonies. The Jesus I know wept when he saw Mary grieving for her brother. 'When Jesus saw her weeping, and the Jews who had come along with her also weeping, he was deeply moved in spirit and troubled. 'Where have you laid him?' he asked. 'Come and see, Lord,' they replied. Jesus wept.'[6]

Even though Jesus knew He was going to raise Lazarus from the dead, He still sat in the messy, middle moment of Mary's pain and was deeply moved. 'Jesus wept' is the shortest verse in the Bible, but it says so much about Jesus' character, about His compassion, about Him not sanitizing our pain and emotions. Strength and stamina for the journey toward our greatest calling requires us to rely on God completely for everything. When we really

> **The Jesus I know wouldn't want a cleaned and sterilized version of our testimonies.**

understand His unfailing love and compassion toward us, we become whole.

> 'Now let Your unfailing love be my comfort,
> in keeping with Your promise to Your servant.
> Shower me with Your compassion so that I may live
> Because I find great joy in Your law.
> Let the proud be humiliated,
> For they sabotage me with a lie;
> Still, I will fix my mind on Your directives.
> Let those who fear You and know Your testimonies
> Come back and find me.
> Let my heart be whole, my record according to what You require
> So that I will not be humiliated.'[7]

Jesus doesn't leave you in those moments of shame as fear causes you to pick at the scabs covering your wounds. He will sit right in the pain with you until you are supernaturally infused with strength, so you can stand victorious with the force of His explosive power flowing in and through you. And in those moments, He reveals His scars to you. The scars that have declared victory over death and pain, over shame and trauma, over humiliation and abandonment, over abuse and betrayal. The scars that heal every wound the hunter, Satan has inflicted upon you so you

> **Jesus doesn't leave you in those moments of shame as fear causes you to pick at the scabs covering your wounds.**

can trust Jesus completely. The scars that show you're strong enough to step into a new season.

PRAYER

Dear Jesus,
I ask You to heal my wounds. Sit with me in the messy middle part of my story as You clean and cleanse my wounding so I can move forward. I pray for protection from unhealthy relationships and the effects of hidden sins within the church. I pray if any of my wounds have been infected by parasites or disease in my wrong thinking, I pray You will use Your disinfectant to clean those wounds thoroughly. I know it will probably sting a little, but it will be better than letting the wounds fester. Help me in the process of learning to forgive others. Show me how much You forgave, even though they hurt You so badly. Soften my edges and help me to become compassionate in why wounded people wound others. I pray for Your strength and stamina to do all this. Amen.

Endnotes: Chapter Ten

Ref 1   Joshua 1:5. Peterson, Eugene H. 2000. *The Message Bible:* Colorado Springs, Colorado. Navpress.

Ref 2   Ephesians 6:10 *The Passion Translation: New Testament with Psalms, Proverbs, and Song of Songs, Second Edition.* Passion & Fire Ministries, Inc. BroadStreet Publishing: 2018.

Ref 3   Exodus 16:3. Ecclesia Bible Society. 2012. *The Voice Bible: Step into the Story of Scripture.* Nashville: Thomas Nelson.

Ref 4   Exodus 16:4. Ecclesia Bible Society. 2012. *The Voice Bible: Step into the Story of Scripture.* Nashville: Thomas Nelson.

Ref 5   Brown, Brené. 2017. *Rising Strong: How the Ability to Reset Transforms the Way We Live, Love, Parent, and Lead.* New York: Random House.

Ref 6   John 11:33-35. Syswerda, Jean, and Faith Organization. 2001. *NIV Women of Faith Study Bible: New International Version.* Grand Rapids, Mich.: Zondervan.

Ref 7   Psalm 119: 76 -80. Ecclesia Bible Society. 2012. *The Voice Bible: Step into the Story of Scripture.* Nashville: Thomas Nelson.

PART THREE

A NEW SEASON

CHAPTER ELEVEN

Recovery of the Elk

'When we spend a lifetime trying to distance ourselves from the parts of our lives that don't fit with who we think we're supposed to be, we stand outside of our story and hustle for our worthiness by constantly performing, perfecting, pleasing, and proving' [1]

BRENÉ BROWN

A wounded elk can survive a hunt if the injury is not fatal, but it must find a safe place to rest and recover. Although I had been healed of all my past wounding, I was still wrestling with the people-pleasing and performance-based stuff, a secondary wound from one of the hunter's more deadly arrows. My best friend called me one day and told me she had booked herself into a Healing Thru Creativity retreat and wondered if I would like to come with her. She said that God had told her to buy an extra ticket for someone and she felt it was for me. At first, I was a little sceptical because to me a healing retreat sounded like new age stuff, but I was curious about the creativity bit. After my friend explained it was a Christian retreat and told me what it was all about, I knew God was prompting me to attend. After making sure my family could cope without me for a couple of days, I packed a bag and headed to the retreat with my friend.

It was a pretty full-on few days and my thoughts of rest at the retreat soon disappeared. Choosing from the sixteen activities they had on offer each day was a challenge and the leader of the programme encouraged everyone to choose something that was outside their creative comfort zone because we may be surprised at what we discover about ourselves and what God wants to reveal to us. I noticed creative writing was on offer and my friend, who is a painter, wanted to attend the session. I knew we needed to come out of our comfort zones, but I wanted to go to some of the sessions with my friend as we had picked totally different things. I told my friend to not tell the leader of the writing session that I was a writer, and she gave me a puzzled look. We had to write as we listened to a piece of music that was played and share, if we wanted to, what we'd written down. My friend encouraged me to share what I'd written, so I did. As raw and unpolished as it was, the piece I had written got an applause from the group and I thanked them for their kindness. The next day I decided I was going to step out of my comfort zone and try some painting in the paint shed. I was going to be doing this session on my own as my friend had already been the day before. Everyone who'd been to the paint shed told everyone to go to a session, so I was

> What was so great about a rickety old paint shed?

a little nervous about this experience. What was so great about a rickety old paint shed?

As I walked up the gravel path toward the paint shed, I began to cry. Why was I getting so emotional? I quickly suppressed the tears because there was no way I was going to have a meltdown around people I'd never met before. A lady gave me a plastic paint smock and directed me to an easel that had a large, blank piece of paper attached to it. I watched others happily painting their 'masterpieces' and chatting to the leader as I was picking up a few tubes of paint and squeezing various colours out ready to paint something, anything that made me focus on what I was going to paint and ignore the tears that were leaking out the corner of my eye. I told God that I was going to control this situation. I was going to perform this task and move onto the next creative activity I had ticked on my list for the day.

The lady said I was to look at the piece of paper and paint what was in my mind. So, with paint brush poised, I waited. After a while, the lady came up to me and asked if I was alright, 'yep' came my short answer as I was trying desperately to find some inspiration. No picture came. So, I waited some more. After what felt like an eternity, something did

I knew that's where I wanted to be. Free. Free from my performance-based mindset. Free from people-pleasing all the time.

come but it wasn't what I expected. It was tears, and lots of them streaming down my face. My feeble attempts to hide them were unsuccessful as I looked up at the splashes of paint along the wooden beams above my head. Different coloured paints that spoke the testimonies of the brush strokes of the people who had gone wild in this paint shed before me. Free to express exactly what they were feeling. I knew that's where I wanted to be. Free. Free from my performance-based mindset. Free from people-pleasing all the time. To tell myself to let go of my control and allow myself to be totally undone by God. I had listened to the lies about myself for too long, telling me I had to perform to feel valued, to be noticed, to feel accepted and affirmed.

The lady came back over to me and asked if she could pray for me. I silently nodded and we stepped outside into the fresh air. Returning to the blank piece of paper, I knew I didn't want to paint 'inside the lines' anymore. I didn't want to always feel like I had to perform to feel loved and valued. God had shown me how much I was worth, and how much He loved me regardless of whether I painted something or not. He told me that He didn't want me to be the Court Jester anymore, performing to please people. He wanted me to know that I was His daughter. I have to tell you that I did end up painting something that day. It wasn't a masterpiece, but to me it was priceless.

Find Your Identity

I don't know what wounds the hunter, Satan have inflicted on you dear friend as he's blood trailed you through the forest, but I do know that I'm not the only one who has struggled with a people-pleasing, performance-based mindset so I feel valued and loved by others. God met me in the most unlikely place to set me free from an identity that was built on lies and He will meet you right here in the pages of this chapter so He can heal your wounds and remind you of your true identity so you can live fully whole. But to find your identity you need to stop running away from yourself.

Luke chapter 15 is the story of the lost son, or prodigal son in some Bible translations and it's about a son who has rebelled and squandered all his father's inheritance. 'With everything spent and nothing left, he grew hungry for there was a severe famine in that land. So, he begged a farmer in that country to hire him. The farmer hired him and sent him out to feed the pigs. The son was so famished, he was willing to even eat the slop given to the pigs, because no one would feed him a thing. Humiliated, the son finally realised what he was doing, and he thought, 'There are many workers at my father's house who have all the food they want with plenty to spare. They lack nothing. Why am I here dying of hunger, feeding these pigs, and eating their slop? I want to go home to my father's house, and say to him, 'Father, I was wrong. I have sinned against you. I'll never be worthy to be called your son. Please, Father, just treat me like one of your employees.' So, the young son set off for home. From a long distance away, his father saw him coming, dressed as a beggar, and great compassion swelled up in his heart for his son who was returning home. So, the father raced out to meet him. He swept him up in his arms, hugged him dearly, and kissed him over and over with tender love. Then the son said, 'Father, I was wrong. I have sinned against you. I could never deserve to be called your son. Just let me be—' The father interrupted and said, 'Son, you're home now!' [2]

> **He can heal your wounds and remind you of your true identity so you can live fully whole.**

The one thing that stands out to me in this story is something we can miss. I find it interesting that we needed to know what the son was wearing when his father saw him coming. The son was dressed as a beggar. So, why put in that detail when the hugging and kissing and welcoming would have driven the point of the story home? Because the son had wrapped himself in an identity that wasn't really who he was. In all his extravagant and reckless living, he possibly became a hustler with the people he hung around. Continually hustling for his worth as his performance-based, people-pleasing, proving made sure that he was deemed worthy of their attention. But the father showed the son that he didn't need to beg and hustle to be worthy of his love. 'Turning to his servants, the father said, 'Quick, bring me the best robe, my very own robe, and I will place it on his shoulders. Bring the ring, the seal of sonship, and I will put it on his finger. And bring out the best shoes you can find for my son. Let's prepare a great feast and celebrate. For this beloved son of mine was once dead, but now he's alive again. Once he was lost, but now he is found!'[3] The father knew the true identity of his son even though he was dressed in beggar's clothes.

> The father knew the true identity of his son even though he was dressed in beggar's clothes.

Walking In Freedom

At the end of the Healing Thru Creativity retreat, we all gathered for the final session where we would share our testimonies of what God had done during the retreat. The creative writing class had been popular, and one of the leaders asked if anyone wanted to share their writing with everyone. A few people got up and read out what they'd written. My friend nudged me in the rib cage and whispered, 'Share what you wrote, Wendy.' I flatly refused. Not because I was afraid to speak in front of about a hundred and fifty people, but because I knew this was a test from God. Was I going to give into my friend's pleas and the few people around me begging me to read out what I'd written? Was I going to people-please my way out of this embarrassing moment as the room became very quiet and all eyes were on me or was, I going to walk in the freedom I'd found in the paint shed?

The leader realised I wasn't going to give into my friend's petitions as it was getting uncomfortable watching us 'kindly' argue with each other and chose someone else to share their story. When the final session was over and we were all making our way to our rooms to collect our bags and say our goodbyes, a gentleman came up to me whom I had met previously in the leatherwork session I had attended, and said, 'You were getting really pressured in reading out your writing weren't you?' I nodded and then smiled, telling him why I believed God had sent me on the retreat and how He had broken off my performance-based, people-pleasing mindset in the paint shed and I knew if I had relented to my friend's request, I would never be free. He smiled looked at me admiringly, and said, 'Well done. That was very brave of you to do that.'

Recovering People-Pleaser

Imagine if you woke up one day and said goodbye to the need of approval? What would that day look like? Would you feel peace?

When you're a recovering people-pleaser like myself, it is a daily choice to say goodbye to the need of approval. Rather than taking the easier option by pleasing people more than God, I find I don't need to hustle for my worth anymore. Paul writes about approval in Galatians 1:10. 'Do you think I am on a mission to please people? If I am still spinning my wheels trying to please men, then there is no way I can be a servant of the Anointed One, the Liberating King.' [4] What's Paul saying when he says, 'spinning my wheels'? He means that he isn't going to waste his time doing things that achieve nothing. As far as Paul was concerned, trying to please men was completely useless. He understood a hard-won truth that he couldn't do the things God told him to do and please men at the same time. If we are to be servants of a liberated King, then we need to be free and liberated from the ineffective work of needing approval all the time because it is this oppressive enslavement that will cause our past wounds to keep bleeding out. However, we cannot swing the approving pendulum the other way and not care less what anyone thinks. That is disconnecting. Paul was saying that he wasn't going to waste energy on pleasing the people who really don't care about him. He knew his true identity was in Christ and He was the One who had willingly laid down His life so everyone, if they choose, could live in freedom.

> *Imagine if you woke up one day and said goodbye to the need of approval?*

Rest and Recovery

Rest and recovery come when we stop running away from our true identity and are brave enough to allow God to heal our wounds. The hunter, Satan has made sure you don't discover your true identity because when you do, you're powerful. He is happy for you to spend a lifetime running away from yourself, so you find no rest from hustling for your worth. Restoration comes when you stop running away. God is still in the business of healing broken hearts and binding up wounds. He is a Father who waits at the gate, searching the horizon for the prodigal to return home again,[5] you just need to stop running away from yourself and run to Him instead.

> **The hunter, Satan has made sure you don't discover your true identity because when you do, you're powerful.**

A few months later after returning from the retreat, I began to feel our family needed to find a safe place to recover completely, to get away and start afresh somewhere else. The paint shed moment had caused me to reflect on everything and I knew I'd come back changed. I sensed it could be time for a shift, a change but I didn't know what. A different role within the leadership perhaps now that I was free from my performance-based mindset? I chatted with my pastor about how I felt. He listened to me and then he said the strangest thing. He told me that maybe I'd outgrown the church. I was a little confused. How can somebody outgrow a church?

I felt the arrow strike.

And it was then that I came to the realisation that I'd put my value and worth in people who had no desire to carry on a relationship with me, leaving me feeling confused, alone and above all else – used. The hunter, Satan had made sure that now I had found my true identity, he was going to wound me with the arrow of offence.

Endnotes: Chapter Eleven

Ref 1   Brown, Brené, 2010. *Gifts of Imperfection: Let Go of Who You Think You're Supposed to Be and Embrace Who You Are.* Minnesota, Hazelden Publishing.

Ref 2   Luke 15:14-21. *The Passion Translation: New Testament with Psalms, Proverbs, and Song of Songs, Second Edition.* Passion & Fire Ministries, Inc. BroadStreet Publishing: 2018.

Ref 3   Luke 15:22-24. *The Passion Translation: New Testament with Psalms, Proverbs, and Song of Songs, Second Edition.* Passion & Fire Ministries, Inc. BroadStreet Publishing: 2018.

Ref 4   Galatians 1:10. Ecclesia Bible Society. 2012. *The Voice Bible: Step into the Story of Scripture.* Nashville: Thomas Nelson.

Ref 5   Wellspring Journal, Daughters of Love and Light. 2021. Adelaide, South Australia.

CHAPTER TWELVE

The Journey Ahead

'To be a Christian means to forgive the inexcusable because God has forgiven the inexcusable in you.' [1]
C.S. LEWIS

The elk is a very adaptable animal which is helpful during the winter months. As the season of warmer months come to an end and deep snow begins to settle on the higher elevation areas, good food and water needs to be found by the elk to survive. Making their way down to lower areas during the winter months, elk can sometimes cover up to twelve miles a day to find vegetation and water to sustain them which helps them to get ready for the spring rutting season.[2] Physiological and behavioural adjustments help elk survive during the winter. Amazingly, an elk rumen in the elk's digestive system produces heat becoming the elk's internal heating system as it breaks down food in the digestion process keeping the elk warm during the cold, winter months.[3]

Our migration to another church and not committing to any leadership roles for over a year, was much needed as I was mentally, emotionally, and physically exhausted from everything I'd gone through. Even though I'd experienced the wounds of rejection and betrayal from the hunter, Satan within the church walls, and I had felt the pain from his arrows and bullets over the years, I still needed the connection a church family gave. Church is not about programs and attending services each and every Sunday, that's not where we'll find the restoration power to heal our broken souls from all the wounding and blood trailing, we have experienced. Healing is found in the blood trail Jesus left behind at the cross, the blood which covers and protects us against the hunter, Satan. However, finding a healthy church where other believers are able to nourish our faith which helps the wounded to stop running, to stop hiding, and to reconnect with the path that was lost when they're so used to being blood trailed by the hunter can sometimes be hard to find. I ran from church for so many years because of wounds. I tried to look for the warmth again, searching for those feelings I had felt when I had had a relationship with Jesus, trying to find the fire of God's presence during the long, long winter of my faith. When we've been wounded, it's hard for us to become vulnerable and find real connection in church because we've put up our walls of protection. So, as a result, we go looking for that sense of belonging

Healing is found in the blood trail Jesus left behind at the cross.

we long for in all the wrong places. The hunter, Satan doesn't want you to find the blood trail of Jesus because 'Satan knows that the blood is the key to his defeat, which is why he works so craftily to remove it from the only place where it may be found – the church.'[4] He wants to shut down the Body, the community of believers because of wounding, of hurts, of betrayal and deep pain so that the restoring path of the blood trail Jesus left behind is covered over, hidden, and never found. The hunter makes sure your faith starves to death in the bleakness of winter before you can find the nourishment that your soul needs because he knows when you feel the warmth of God's presence from a real community, when you are fed on the bread of an authentic communion, and you observe legitimate believers drinking from His covenant cup and keep on remembering Him, then the path to His redeeming blood trail will illuminate your way home because 'when people are living like Jesus, there will be blood on the floor. There will be a thousand little deaths.'[5] A people who have learned to die daily to their selves and have chosen to walk with the Spirit, keeping in step and in sync with God's Spirit because they set aside self-interests and work together to create true community instead of a culture consumed by provocation, pride, and envy.[6]

Helpless in His Nail-Scarred Hands

Elks are social animals and learn migration routes from their mother and other members of the herd. Over the generations, elks will use the same winter route year after year, following the same paths to familiar surroundings knowing it will provide them food, water, and shelter from the harsh winter. Elks stay close to each other during winter, sharing food in the areas where the snow is shallow which increases their chance of surviving during the harsh, winter months.[7] Do this in remembrance of Me,[8] Jesus instructs His disciples at the last supper. Drink from My cup of suffering, reminding wounded, broken souls that He was wounded first. He gives thanks for the 'two visible symbols: bread and wine. Bread to tell of my broken body, He said, and wine to tell of my shed blood. And as often as you meet together, the world wonders what you're doing and peeks in to see, and they see you eating the bread and drinking the wine, and you're thinking of me.'[9] The same path, the familiar surroundings, day after day, week after week, month after month, year after year. It takes courage and boldness to follow the path that flows with the redemptive blood trail because it requires us to show our abandonment wounds and surrender them to Him. It takes bravery to become helpless in His nail-scarred hands.

> **It takes courage and boldness to follow the path that flows with the redemptive blood trail...**
>
> **it takes bravery to become helpless in His nail-scarred hands.**

A Drink Offering

The Apostle Paul was being poured out as a drink offering as he felt the cold, harsh feeling of being abandoned and deserted by others. He uses this term in 2 Timothy 4:6 to parallel with the Old Testament tradition of pouring a small cup of wine around the base of the altar where an animal was being sacrificed. The wine was to represent the thankfulness of the worshipper.[10] Paul drinks the wine of surrender willingly as he knows his time is short and his departure in this life is nearing. Paul writes about his hardships from his prison cell, lamenting towards the end of his letter of the abandonment he's feeling because his friends have deserted him. In his suffering, he proclaims that even though no one defended or supported him, he doesn't hold those things against them and asks young Timothy to bring his cloak and scrolls, especially the parchments. Winter was a dangerous time to travel across the Mediterranean Sea, and Paul knew Timothy needed to try his best to come visit him before winter blew in. 'On your way here, pick up the cloak I left with Carpus in Troas, and bring the scrolls – especially the parchments...Try to come before winter blows in.'[11] Paul perhaps needs these things for a sense of comfort from his friend's thoughtlessness as he awaited his execution. Perhaps, like Paul, your faith has been tested by the icy winter winds of desertion and abandonment that have tried to extinguish the warmth of God's presence that can be felt in real, genuine friendships.

The hunter, Satan wants you to fall for the lie that yes, you are alone, you are abandoned, and unwanted. He'll whisper that church people are dopey, dormant, and debilitated and are never to be trusted with your heart. He'll remind you of all the times you tried to gain warmth in their embrace to help you through the winter months, only to feel their cold shoulder and icy judgments toward you. So, your wounds bleed out, you keep on running, you keep on feeling emotionally and physically drained and your faith becomes malnourished and worn out looking for the blades of grass

> **The hunter, Satan wants you to fall for the lie that yes, you are alone, you are abandoned, and unwanted.**

underneath the snowfall of not meeting together because they've flaked out on you, they've fallen asleep, leaving you searching, longing for a real community of believers where everyone eats the bread and drinks the wine and remembers how Jesus felt when His friends said they'd be there for Him, but they fell asleep instead, leaving Jesus alone and abandoned for the journey ahead.

The Journey Ahead

The Garden of Gethsemane is where Jesus went with His disciples after the Passover meal. He asks them to stay awake and stand and watch as it customary to not fall asleep on Passover night so you could speak of God's redemption, and according to Jewish teaching, if anyone fell asleep during this time the group was thereby dissolved.[12]

The stinging wound of abandonment is felt by Jesus. The first sip from the cup of wrath and suffering, 'tasting in His soul the contents…and in a few hours, at the cross, He will drain it to its dregs.'[13] He prays, 'Father, this is the last thing I want. If there is any way, please take this bitter cup from Me.'[14] He sweats blood, the first drops fall to the ground[15] to start the blood trail that leads us all toward our healing, our restoration, our redemption. 'Not My will, but Yours be done.'[16] The trial became the trail. The drops of blood we choose to follow when we've felt

> **The trial became the trail.**

the stinging wounds of abandonment. Don't give up now, dear friend, find a community who eats the bread and drinks the wine. A Body of believers who are willing to provide you food, water, and shelter from the harshness of winter. Feel the warmth of real friendships that keeps you going for the journey ahead. All because they remember Him.

Endnotes: Chapter Twelve

Ref 1   Internet search. C.S. Lewis quotes.

Ref 2   petseatable.com/do-elk-migrate. Post by Lena J. Roling February 22, 2022.

Ref 3   huntwildpa.com/2019/03/06/how-elk-handle-winter

Ref 4   Winkler, Kyle. 2001. *Silence Satan: Shutting Down the Enemy's Attacks, Threats, Lies, and Accusations.* Charisma House, Lake Mary, Florida. Published by Passio.

Ref 5   Voskamp, Ann. 2016. *The Broken Way: A Daring Path to the Abundant Life.* Grand Rapids, Michigan: Zondervan.

Ref 6   Galatians 5:25-26. Ecclesia Bible Society. 2012. *The Voice Bible: Step into the Story of Scripture.* Nashville: Thomas Nelson.

Ref 7   BEHAVE \Stories of applied animal behaviour. Surviving winter in the face of habitat loss: biological constraints of Elk and deer. By Jeff Manning. Winter foraging by deer and elk – University of Idaho.

Ref 8   Luke 22:19. Syswerda, Jean, and Faith Organization. 2001. *NIV Women of Faith Study Bible: New International Version.* Grand Rapids, Mich.: Zondervan.

Ref 9   Tozer, A.W, James L. Snyder. *The Fire of God's Presence: Drawing Near to a Holy God.* 2020. Bethany House Publishers, Minnesota, USA.

Ref 10   'Drink Offerings' commentary. Syswerda, Jean, and Faith Organization. 2001. *NIV Women of Faith Study Bible: New International Version.* Grand Rapids, Mich.: Zondervan.

Ref 11   2 Timothy 4:12-21 Ecclesia Bible Society. 2012. *The Voice Bible: Step into the Story of Scripture.* Nashville: Thomas Nelson.

Ref 12   Keener, Craig S. 1993. *The IVP Bible Background Commentary: New Testament.* Downers Grove, Ill. InterVarsity Press.

Ref 13   McKinley, Mike. *Passion: How Christ's Final Day Changes Your Every Day.* 2013. The Good Book Company.

Ref 14   Matthew 26:39. Ecclesia Bible Society. 2012. *The Voice Bible: Step into the Story of Scripture.* Nashville: Thomas Nelson.

Ref 15   Luke 22:44 Syswerda, Jean, and Faith Organization. 2001. *NIV Women of Faith Study Bible: New International Version.* Grand Rapids, Mich.: Zondervan.

Ref 16   Matthew 26:42. Ecclesia Bible Society. 2012. *The Voice Bible: Step into the Story of Scripture.* Nashville: Thomas Nelson.

CHAPTER THIRTEEN

Wallowing in the Mud

'*Roll the credits on the stories that are done.*' [1]
DONALD MILLER

An elk wallow is created by a bull elk finding a pool of water, digging into the ground with his hooves and antlers to push up the dirt, urinating into it and then rolling in it. As gross as this may sound, wallowing in this wet, muddy 'odorous creation'[2] to attract females is the bull elk's way of sending a clear message to all cows letting them know that his pheromone – soaked, perfumed coat [2] along with his bugle calls mean he's ready for action as the rutting season approaches. A smart hunter will search for a wallowing hole a couple of weeks prior to the mating process begins as this is the crucial time the bull starts to gather his harem of cows. Hiding in nearby trees for cover, the hunter can set up his spot by cutting into branches to create a shooting lane and ambush the bull elk while he is busy wallowing. As long as the hunter makes sure that the cover spot is in range and the wind is blowing in a direction away from himself (as a bull elk is more likely to sniff him out) then the odds are in the hunter's favour.[3]

Like the bull elk, we too can wallow in the mud of our past offenses. We roll around and around in the muddy, repugnant odour of every infraction and wrongdoing covering ourselves in the stench of what other people have done to us, hoping to gain a harem of followers that becomes a herd. Sadly, if you've been in church for any length of time you can spot a wallowing hole rather quickly. You'll find every bruised and bitter soul covering themselves in the mud of gossip and slanderous comments, hoping it will attract others as the vengeful perfume divides up the Body of Christ rather than keeping the Body unified. I know, I was that person. I rolled many times in the wallowing hole of self-pity believing that my complaints about my past hurts were justified. However, wallowing is dangerous for our spiritual growth because while we're rolling around in the wet mud, discharging all our toxic waste the hunter, Satan is setting up a shooting lane ready to take a shot at you and start a blood trail. If we're too busy wallowing over our offenses, then the enemy goes unnoticed, and he can easily ambush you causing you to run and leave a blood trail.

Spiritual Vagabonds

According to Merriam-Webster's dictionary a vagabond is a person who wanders from place to place without a fixed home: one leading a vagabond life.[4] Wallowers tend to be wanderers roaming around from church to church because of past offenses and the hunter, Satan will use all our indulgent feelings of hopelessness to his advantage, keeping the blood trail going from one church to the other. Don't get me wrong, I am not saying that being mistreated by others is okay, far from it. But what I am saying is that if we want to be free from the blood trail that flows behind us, then we need to find the path that has a blood trail which leads us to the cross.

Looking back at my own story, I can see where I sometimes reacted out of immaturity in my faith because of offense. I didn't really understand the whole humility, and how we need to die to ourselves daily, discipleship concepts that help us to surrender to Christ. In the past, a mentor tried to caution me because I was running along the path of pride, however, I chose to ignore their wise counsel and carried on rolling in the mud of offense. As a child, I had watched my parents on a number of occasions become offended and leave during the middle of a church service, so I wasn't taught that sometimes, as loving believers, we need to work through our differences, bringing unity rather than division. Jesus wants us to stop wallowing in the mud of offenses so He can heal our wounds because He knows that Satan wants you to become a spiritual vagabond like himself so he can continue to blood trail you. In Job 1:7, God asks the accuser where he's been. 'Oh, roaming here and there, running about the earth and observing its inhabitants.'[5] That's what the hunter does, he observes you from the covering of his shooting lane in the forest trees as you wallow in your offenses. If we want to turn our wounds into scars and step into the future God has for us, we need to quit rolling around in the sludge and slush of gossip and

> Jesus wants us to stop wallowing in the mud of offenses so He can heal our wounds.

slander by developing a maturity in our faith walk. Discipleship is the key motivator in our faith for our growth, so we are built up until we all reach unity in the faith and in the knowledge of the Son of God and become mature, attaining to the whole measure of the fullness of Christ.[6]

Churches will never be perfect because its Body is made up of people. However, the wounds inflicted on others can be devastating and painful causing us to wallow in our anger and hurt. But I have found that the more I keep surrendering my brokenness to Jesus, the more the strong emotions attached to my scars start to fade. Once we stop bathing our wounds in the stench of past offenses, the sooner we can become the Repairers of the Breach and the Restorers of Streets to Dwell In, which Isaiah speaks about. But we need to take away the yoke from our midst, stop pointing our fingers and quit playing the blame game. Like you, I have been badly wounded by the hunter, Satan, however, I don't want to be a wallower anymore! God is judge and I have learned to leave all the judging up to Him when someone tries to offend me. Revelation 22:14 promises that those who wash their garments are blessed and, in the end, they have rightful access to the tree of life and will enter the city through its gates.[8] I choose to keep my garments clean because I want access to the tree of life.

Lies and deception are what hunters use to trap elks and wound them so they can create an exciting blood trail through the forest. Many offenses have caused me to become wounded and, on the run, but the wallowing hole is not where God wants me to be, and He doesn't want you there either. When we choose to stop rolling around in our past offenses of hurts, pain, and disappointments and follow the blood trail that leads us to the cross of Cavalry, we will realise that Jesus took the punishment for our suffering and pain. Wallowing isn't for you, dear friend, if you want to see those wounds of offense healed. We're all unfinished projects and struggle from time to time with offenses. We need to really believe that He who began a good work in you will carry it on to completion until the day of Christ Jesus. [9] As Donald Miller states, 'Roll the credits on the stories that are done.' Stop reading the long list of the cast and crew that offended you in a movie you no longer play a part in. And if that doesn't stop you rolling around in the wallowing hole, Isaiah 53:7-9 is proof that the crucifixion of Jesus heals every wound because we've all done our own thing, gone our own way. And God has piled all our sins, everything we've done wrong, on Him, on Him. He was beaten, He was tortured, but He didn't say a word. Like a lamb taken to be slaughtered and like a sheep being sheared, he took it all in silence. Justice miscarried, and He was led off – and did anyone really know what was happening? He died without a thought for His own welfare, beaten bloody for the sins of my people. They buried Him with the wicked, threw Him in a grave with a rich man, even though He'd never hurt a soul or said one word that wasn't true.'[10] He did all that so we could stay out of the wallowing hole and be healed from all our wounding.

PRAYER

Dear Jesus,
I don't want to wallow in offense anymore. I lay every offense that has caused wounding at the foot of the cross and ask You to make my garments clean. I don't want to be a Spiritual vagabond anymore. When I've felt abandoned, I know that You, Jesus, have never abandoned me,

You never left my side. Please show me how to become a repairer and a restorer and build up people instead of tearing them down because of the bitterness and unforgiveness that comes with the wounds of offense. Let me feel the warmth of real, trusted friendships that keep me going along the journey ahead of me, and help me to follow the path that flows with Your redemptive blood trail. Amen.

Endnotes: Chapter Thirteen

Ref 1   Dream Big Podcast with Bob Goff and Friends. Interview with Donald Miller.

Ref 2   rmef.org 'Scouting report: wallow your way to an elk.' By Mark Kayser (Rocky Mountain Elk Foundation)

Ref 3   Go Hunt/ Tips for hunting elk on wallows Sep 17, 2020 YouTube video.

Ref 4   Merriam-Webster.com 'vagabond'

Ref 5   Job 1:7 Ecclesia Bible Society. 2012. *The Voice Bible: Step into the Story of Scripture.* Nashville: Thomas Nelson.

Ref 6   Ephesians 4:13. Syswerda, Jean, and Faith Organization. 2001. *NIV Women of Faith Study Bible: New International Version.* Grand Rapids, Mich.: Zondervan.

Ref 7   Isaiah 58:9-12 *Spiritual Warfare Bible, NKJV.* 2012. Lake Mary, Florida, Charisma House

Ref 8   Revelation 22:14. Ecclesia Bible Society. 2012. *The Voice Bible: Step into the Story of Scripture.* Nashville: Thomas Nelson.

Ref 9   Philippians 1:6. Syswerda, Jean, and Faith Organization. 2001. *NIV Women of Faith Study Bible: New International Version.* Grand Rapids, Mich.: Zondervan.

Ref 10   Isaiah 53:7-9. Peterson, Eugene H. 2000. *The Message Bible:* Colorado Springs, Colorado. Navpress.

PART FOUR

FOLLOWING THE BLOOD TRAIL OF JESUS

CHAPTER FOURTEEN

Last Seen Spot

'Free, for the freedom of others.' [1]
BOBBIE HOUSTON

I know what you're thinking. All this talk about hunting, running, blood trailing, ruts and the uncanny parallels between wounded Christians and the North American bull elk are helpful, but how can the worst pain lead you into your greatest calling? How can we stop the hunter, Satan from causing us to be wounded and on the run? Well, there are weapons we get to use that make sure we don't end up being blood trailed through our forest of pain again. Learning how to not *leave* a blood trail but to *follow* a blood trail is key to your faith surviving because finding the path to freedom will do us no good at all if we keep on making the same mistakes over and over again. God has a plan and a purpose for your life and the last part of this book is dedicated to empowering and equipping you to follow the One who's blood trail can set you free completely.

Most hunters give up the chase if they lose the blood trail of an elk. This signals that the animal has stopped bleeding out and is recovering from its wounding. But a hunter who is determined to find the wounded elk needs to find the last seen spot where he found blood so he can figure out which way the elk ran. Wallowing in the mud and poking at your pain-filled wounds won't help your wounds to heal because they'll just bleed out again. They need to turn into valuable scars so the hunter, Satan cannot track you down. But how do wounds turn into scars and how are we led into our greatest calling?

How can we stop the hunter, Satan from causing us to be wounded and on the run?

Reconciliation and restoration needs to happen first, and it is found in a place that the hunter, Satan doesn't want you to find. All those broad, well-worn paths that led you around in circles or toward a dead end have the hoof prints that have been left by many wounded elks who decided for one reason, or another that they would rather keep on running than to find the path to safety, to freedom, to home. As I said at the start of this book, you can only move forward, and the Psalmist writes about two paths in Psalm 139.

> 'God, I invite your searching gaze into my heart.
> Examine me through and through;
> find out everything that may be hidden within me.
> Put me to the test and sift through all my anxious cares.
> See if there is *any path* of pain I'm walking on,
> and lead me back to your glorious, everlasting ways –
> *the path* that brings me back to you.'[2] (emphasis mine)

When You're Lost, He's the One to Follow

You've been sifted by the hunter, Satan for far too long, so why would you willingly let God sift through all your anxious cares? Pride and stubbornness only keeps us running in the wrong direction, and the Any Path is a journey that is only filled with more heartache and pain. I understand, you've been hurt, and you believe that all that poking, and prodding will inflict more pain on you than if you never had found this cabin in the forest and rested awhile. However, Jesus quite clearly states that He is *the* path, *the* Way when you're lost and there is no other One to follow.³ If we truly want to be free from the pain of our past and be led back to His glorious and everlasting ways, we need to find the blood trail that leads us back to Him. Trust me, it won't be long before your wounds start to bleed out again and the hunter, Satan tracks you down.

> **We need to find the blood trail that leads us back to Him.**

At the start of this book, I mentioned that God wanted me to build something for you. Something that you could easily find as you searched for a clearing and the way through your forest of pain. A little wooden cabin that welcomed you. A place where you were able to take off your muddied shoes and make yourself at home, so you could catch your breath for a moment. Perhaps as you passed under the 'welcome' sign above the door frame where a cosy chair in which to rest your weary soul was waiting for you, you didn't take much notice of the doorway as you entered in. Maybe you were in too much pain from your wounding to care that the doorway wasn't wide, bejewelled and decorated, but a doorway that was plain, unassuming, and narrow.[4] And in that moment of your anguish, fear, and despair you knew that you needed Someone to be moved with compassion to help you. Someone who doesn't just patch up your wounds and say, 'good job for resting awhile, now keep running' but Someone who is willing to take all your brokenness and pour olive oil into those infected wounds and heal them once and for all.

The parable of the good Samaritan is well known whether you're a believer or not because the principles in the story are deeply ingrained in each one of us on some level. The parable is found in Luke 10:30-36 and Jesus starts the story with a Jewish man who has been robbed and left for dead. Two religious people see the Jewish man bleeding and in a critical condition but chose to walk by him. Jesus then brings the story to its conclusion.

> And in that moment of your anguish, fear, and despair you knew that you needed Someone to be moved with compassion to help you.

'Finally, another man, a Samaritan, came upon the bleeding man and was moved with tender compassion for him. He stooped down and gave him first aid, pouring olive oil on his wounds, disinfecting them with wine, and bandaging them to stop the bleeding. Lifting him up, he placed him on his own donkey and brought him to an inn. Then he took him from his donkey and carried him to a room for the night. The next morning, he took his own money from his wallet and gave it to the innkeeper with these words: 'Take care of him until I come back from my journey. If it costs more than this, I will repay you when I return.'

When we're wounded, we hope that religious people see us and take care of our wounds, only to be left half-dead and disappointed, feeling even more hurt because they chose to walk by. Thank goodness Jesus didn't think the same when He saw our wounded condition, choosing to commit Himself to our restoration in the Garden of Gethsemane (which means oil press) and then poured Himself out for us on the cross, regardless of whether we were deserving of His help. Jesus was so moved with compassion that His blood became the disinfecting wine that can be poured into every infectious wound we've experienced. Jesus left a blood trail on the cross for you and me to follow that has the power to clean our wounds and mend our broken hearts. It didn't cost Him something, like the good Samaritan, it cost him everything.

> **The last seen spot of your blood trail the hunter, Satan has been following ends right here.**

And once you discover the path and start to follow the blood trail of the One who was wounded first, you'll discover your greatest calling which is to find salvation in Christ and to live a life that shines His light. This is where your blood trailing finishes. The last seen spot of your blood trail the hunter, Satan has been following ends right here.

Follow the Blood Trail

As I mentioned at the start of this chapter, learning how to not leave a blood trail but to follow a blood trail is key to your faith surviving. Unfortunately, I cannot promise that the hunter, Satan won't find you again. He is relentless in reminding you of every sin and every failure, so you start running again. But he cannot wound you with his weapons anymore because Jesus stripped him of them. Now is the time to rise up dear friend because Colossians 2:14-15 gives us the courage to fight back and stand our ground. 'He erased it all – our sins, our stained soul – he deleted it all and they cannot be retrieved! Everything we once were in Adam has been placed onto His cross and nailed permanently there as a public display of cancellation. Then Jesus made a public spectacle of all the powers and principalities of darkness, stripping away from them every weapon and all their spiritual authority and power to accuse us. And by the power of the cross, Jesus led then around as prisoners in a procession of triumph. He was not their prisoner; they were his!'[5] This knowledge is what the hunter, Satan doesn't want you to know. He doesn't want you to find out that Jesus stripped him of every weapon and all his spiritual authority. He cannot bear for you to know that your training and equipping of your weapons started at the Last Supper in Matthew 26:26-28 when Jesus took the bread, gave thanks, and

> **This knowledge is what the hunter, Satan doesn't want you to know. He doesn't want you to find out that Jesus stripped him of every weapon and all his spiritual authority.**

broke it, and gave it to His disciples, saying, 'Take eat; this is My body.' Then he took the cup, gave thanks, and offered it to them, saying, 'Drink from it, all of you. This is My blood of the covenant which is poured out for many for the forgiveness of sins.'[6]

A few years ago, I discovered the power that was found in taking communion every day, and over the years of taking communion regularly I have been astonished at the things God has been doing in my life. It all started when I got a phone call from my dad after my mum had been for a routine mammogram and they had got the results. The doctor had found a lump and told my mum that she had breast cancer. I was shocked and upset and I told my dad we needed to contact my sister who still lives in England, as my parents had emigrated to Australia a few years previously. I told my sad news to the connect group the following week and knew we needed to pray for my mum. One lady suggested I start taking communion every day for my mum's healing. I took communion at church, but never really thought about taking it every day at home. So, I brought some crackers and blackcurrant juice and took communion each morning after breakfast. My mum was scheduled for the lump to be removed from her breast and a course of chemotherapy to follow. As I was walking alongside mum through her treatment, I finally knew how much my parents really did love and appreciate me, even though they rarely verbalised it. While I was helping my parents, we found out our friend from church had a tumour on her liver. She hadn't been well for a while and now we knew the cause. I found myself walking alongside both women through their operations and

> **I discovered the power that was found in taking communion every day.**

treatment as I continued to take communion for them each day. I was beginning to understand the scarlet thread I was following along the path was not only covering my mum and my friend, but it was healing all my wounds too. The wounds from my performance-based mindset, and the sting of rejection, to the abandonment I felt in my childhood were being turned into valuable scars so I could help others discover the power of these weapons found in communion. Thanks to Jesus, Cancer was disarmed at the cross, and after a long road of gruelling treatment and watching the effects from it, my mum, and my friend were both healed and restored back to full health. It was now clear to me, without a shadow of a doubt, that the healing power of the blood trail Jesus left behind at the cross is where our worst pain leads us into our greatest calling which is to find salvation in Christ. It is in His salvation that we find healing from all our wounding and the restoration that delivers us completely. We find the assurance of His deliverance, His liberation, His restoration, and His redemption which strengthens us to live a life that fully shines His light.

> **It is in His salvation that we find healing from all our wounding and the restoration that delivers us completely.**

Endnotes: Chapter Fourteen.

Ref 1   The Friendship Table with Bobbie and Friends. Hillsong Sisterhood. 2021

Ref 2   Psalm 139:23-24. *The Passion Translation: New Testament with Psalms, Proverbs, and Song of Songs, Second Edition.* Passion & Fire Ministries, Inc. BroadStreet Publishing: 2018.

Ref 3   John 14:6. Syswerda, Jean, and Faith Organization. 2001. *NIV Women of Faith Study Bible: New International Version.* Grand Rapids, Mich.: Zondervan.

Ref 4   Matthew 7:13. Ecclesia Bible Society. 2012. *The Voice Bible: Step into the Story of Scripture.* Nashville: Thomas Nelson.

Ref 5   Colossians 2:14-15. *The Passion Translation: New Testament with Psalms, Proverbs, and Song of Songs, Second Edition.* Passion & Fire Ministries, Inc. BroadStreet Publishing: 2018.

Ref 6   Matthew 26:26-28. Syswerda, Jean, and Faith Organization. 2001. *NIV Women of Faith Study Bible: New International Version.* Grand Rapids, Mich.: Zondervan.

CHAPTER FIFTEEN

The Downed Elk

'*Satan never wastes a fiery dart on an area covered in armour.*' [1]
BETH MOORE

Hunters work hard to track an elk through blood trailing and he needs to ensure the elk is dead before he can go near it, so preparing a follow-up shot is essential. Patience is needed by the hunter to allow the elk time to succumb to its wounding and take its last breath. Broken off tree branches and dirt that has been kicked up are signs that the wounded elk could be close by and so the hunter needs to proceed with stealth and caution. The worst thing that can happen for a hunter is to watch a downed elk they thought was dead, rise up and escape back into the forest.[2]

The Follow-up Shot

Ever since he deceived man in the garden, Satan has done his very best to afflict us with his arrows and shots so that we hide from God, and eventually run away from the very One who loved us first. So, what could be worse than Satan doing all the hard work over his three-year plan to send Jesus to the cross, only to discover that all the wounding Jesus endured, all the pain He suffered, every arrow of affliction that Satan shot at Him during His crucifixion he forgot something. As far as Satan was concerned Jesus was finally dead. No more Jesus meant victory was his. Now his rebellion was complete. However, this skilled, experienced hunter forgot one essential part of his plan to take Jesus down. He failed to prepare a follow-up shot. And as he watched Jesus rise up out of the tomb on the third day, Satan must have broken into a cold sweat because he knew that the worst pain he had inflicted on Jesus, the worst wounding Jesus had encountered from all Satan's weapons to take Him out, had actually led Jesus to His greatest calling, to open up the path of the blood trail for our salvation. This thought gives every wounded elk hope. It reminds us that all the wounding the hunter, Satan inflicted upon us wasn't for nothing. All those painful moments haven't been wasted because as I have discovered in my own life, the worst pain you've gone through can lead you into your greatest calling which is salvation in Christ Jesus.

> **The worst pain you've gone through can lead you into your greatest calling which is salvation in Christ Jesus.**

Reading a Shopping List

My warrior princess spirit always loved reading about the armour of God Paul spoke about in Ephesians chapter 6. 'Putting on' the whole armour brought visions to my imagination of believers on battlefields, fighting off the principalities, powers, rulers of darkness, and spiritual forces of wickedness that came against them. All that said, I would still read through each piece of God's armour like I was reading a shopping list. 'Don't forget the helmet, sword, shoes, breastplate, belt, and shield, along with the eggs, milk and bread, okay Wendy?' You may smile, but if we don't get a handle on why we need each and every piece of God's armour and what it represents instead of just reeling it off like a daily shopping list, it won't help us become victors over further wounding and the hunter, Satan will wound us over and over again and start another blood trail for him to follow. All our pain we experienced will be for nothing, and our wounds will never turn into victorious scars that lead us into our greatest calling which is to live in the salvation of Christ. This is one of the reasons why I wrote this book, it is not just about dealing with our wounding and to help you stop running, it's about getting back up when the hunter, Satan believes he's got the victory over you. It's

> **It's about getting back up when the hunter, Satan believes he's got the victory over you.**

about making sure the hunter, Satan doesn't take you out with a follow-up shot.

'We Don't Die in the End Like the Elk, Do We?!'

When I shared my book proposal with my friend, the first thing she said was, 'Oh no, we don't die in the end like the elk, do we?!' At first, I reminded her that this book wasn't about dying or death or our demise, but one of redemption, life, salvation, and resurrection. But the more I thought about my friend's comment, the more I thought about the crucifixion and the death of Jesus and His resurrection from the sealed tomb. A lightbulb moment of clarification happened in my mind, and I suddenly realised that, yes, dying to ourselves is what we need to do! In 2 Corinthians 4:8-10 Paul writes about being discouraged but triumphant. 'We are hard-pressed on every side, yet not crushed; we are perplexed, but not in despair; persecuted, but not forsaken; struck down, but not destroyed – always carrying about in the body the dying of the Lord Jesus, that the life of Jesus also may be manifested in our body.'[3] Paul's description implies we are carrying Jesus' death around like pallbearers carrying a casket when we are afflicted.[4] Jesus became the suffering servant and willingly went to the cross to die for us so that the hunter, Satan could no longer claim victory over us.

> Yes, dying to ourselves is what we need to do!

If we use the allegory of the elk, we can see that Jesus became the downed elk in our place so that death could be conquered once and for all. The One that the prophet Isaiah describes as a 'man of sorrows...who bore our griefs and carried our sorrows... was wounded for our transgressions... bruised for our iniquities.'[5] How was Jesus able to defeat Satan? He used every single piece of armour as He went to the cross! He was showing us *how* to use every piece right throughout His trial, pain, wounding, and crucifixion to deflect the hunter's arrows and shots which are all designed and fashioned to cause the death of our faith which in turn causes the death of our relationship with God. What if we didn't just 'click on' God's armour but shielded ourselves in it from head to toe so every piece deflected the hunter's arrows and shots that try to penetrate our faith?

> What if we didn't just 'click on' God's armour but shielded ourselves in it from head to toe...

The Whole Armour

Let's read about the whole armour of God in Ephesians 6:10-20, shall we?

'Finally, my brethren, be strong in the Lord and in the power of His might. Put on the whole armour of God, that you may be able to stand against the wiles of the devil. For we do not wrestle against flesh and blood, but against principalities, against powers, against rulers of the darkness of this age, against spiritual hosts of wickedness in the heavenly places. Therefore, take up the whole armour of God, that you may be able to withstand in the evil day, and having done all, to stand. Stand therefore, having girded your waist with truth, having put on the breastplate of righteousness, and having shod your feet with the preparation of the gospel of peace; above all, taking the Shield of Faith with which, you will be able to quench all the fiery darts of the wicked one. And take the helmet of salvation, and the sword of the Spirit, which is the word of God; praying always with all prayer and supplication in the Spirit, being watchful to this end with all perseverance and supplication for all the saints – and for me, that I may open my mouth boldly to make known the mystery of the gospel, for which I am an ambassador in chains; that in it I may speak boldly, as I ought to speak.'6

When we understand that people, flesh, and blood, are not our enemies that have wounded us and caused us pain, but the principalities, powers, rulers of the darkness of this age, spiritual hosts of wickedness in the heavenly places behind the wounding we will be able to clearly see the hunter, Satan's schemes.

Helmet of Hope

So, dear friend, let's get you armoured up and ready for hunting season, shall we? We will start with fitting you first with the Helmet of Salvation. 'Salvation is to the soul what the head is to the body – the principal thing it should labour to secure; and hope is to our salvation what the helmet is to the head'7 reminds puritan, William Gurnall. If the hunter, Satan can take you out with a head shot, then he will. His amnesia arrows can sink all too easily into our thin-skinned thinking, making us forget who God says we are unless the Helmet of

Salvation is a snug, secure, tight fit on our heads. Our confidence is found in our hope of our confession. 'So, friends, we can now – without hesitation – walk right up to God, into 'the Holy place.' Jesus has cleared the way by the blood of his sacrifice, acting as our priest before God. The 'curtain' into God's presence is His body. So, let's do it – full of belief, confident that we're presentable inside and out. Let's keep a firm grip on the promises that keep us going.'[8] Jesus has cleared the trees in your forest of pain dear, wounded friend, so you can follow His blood trail right into the presence of God. The Helmet of Salvation gives us an assurance of our hope in the promises of God's Word, helping us to understand that no matter what anyone says about us, our confidence and affirmation is found in who God says we are. Sadly, I believe Satan knows more scripture verses about the hope of our salvation and our identity in Christ than some believers do because he seems to be very good at starting his conversations with a question that circles back to what God has said, and if we don't know God's Word, our identity, and the hope of our salvation then the hunter's arrows of accusation will knock an unsecured Helmet right off our heads.

> If we don't know God's Word, our identity, and the hope of our salvation then the hunter's arrows of accusation will knock an unsecured Helmet right off our heads.

It Is Written

In Matthew chapter 4 we find Satan trying to undermine Jesus' identity and authority by tempting Him while He was in the wilderness. 'If you are the Son of God...' was Satan's loaded weapon to drain Jesus of His identity, authority, and confidence. Unlike Eve, Jesus didn't misquote God's Word and add something that God didn't say. The arrows tips covered in false accusation just bounced right off Jesus when He shot back with 'For it is written...' [9] causing the hunter to withdraw back to his camp rather quickly. Time and time again we read of Jesus' authority and identity being questioned right throughout His three-year ministry, and the accusations just

> The arrows tips covered in false accusation just bounced right off Jesus.

kept coming when He was arrested and taken into custody by the chief priests who gathered witnesses to falsely accuse and distort Jesus' identity so they could accuse Him and put Him to death. 'Do You have anything to say in Your own defence? What do You think of what all these people have said about You?' [10] asks the High Priest. Jesus' identity was again being scrutinised, but Jesus didn't say a word. Even though He was spat upon, slapped, punched, mocked, and humiliated, Jesus took it all because no matter what anyone said about Him, He knew Who He was. His sense of worth didn't come from other people's opinions of Him, only God's opinion counted.

Wounding comes when we allow the arrows of accusations from the hunter, Satan's bow and other people's opinions of who they think we are to penetrate our thinking. 'For you, the Eternal's Word is your happiness. It is your focus – from dusk to dawn'[11] pens the Psalmist. I realise now that if I'd made the Eternal's Word my happiness and strapped up the Helmet of

Salvation, secured the hope of the promises and the truth of God's Word to my thinking, then the bullets that wounded me so badly when I was fifteen from the reverend would not have penetrated so deeply into my soul.

Of course, I cannot change the past, but I can help and guide you, dear wounded friend, by making sure your Helmet of Salvation, the hope of God's promises on which you need to cling to is securely fixed. Our value and worth comes from God and Him only because as Stanley J. Grenz points out 'We spend so much time and expend so much energy trying to gain a sense of worth from others. In the end, however, our value is not based on how others perceive our worth. Ultimately, only God's opinion of us matters.' [12] Arrows of accusations? Bullying bullets of lies? Don't wait for the hunter's follow- up shot to take you out. Rise up again downed elk and run with the confidence of the hope of your salvation!

> Rise up again downed elk and run with the confidence of the hope of your salvation!

Endnotes: Chapter Fifteen

Ref 1   Beth Moore. Instagram post.

Ref 2   realtree.com/big-game-hunting-articles/how-to-recover-a-wounded-elk

Ref 3   2 Corinthians 4:8-10. *Spiritual Warfare Bible, NKJV.* 2012. Lake Mary, Florida, Charisma House

Ref 4   Keener, Craig S. 1993. *The IVP Bible Background Commentary: New Testament.* Downers Grove, Ill. InterVarsity Press.

Ref 5   Isaiah 53:3-5. *Spiritual Warfare Bible, NKJV.* 2012. Lake Mary, Florida, Charisma House

Ref 6   Ephesians 6: 10-20. *Spiritual Warfare Bible, NKJV.* 2012. Lake Mary, Florida, Charisma House

Ref 7   Gurnall, William. 2010. *The Christian in Complete Armour.* Peabody, Mass.: Hendrickson ; Edinburgh.

Ref 8   Hebrews 10 19-21. Peterson, Eugene H. 2000. *The Message Bible:* Colorado Springs, Colorado. Navpress.

Ref 9   Matthew 4:3 and Matthew 4:10. *Spiritual Warfare Bible, NKJV.* 2012. Lake Mary, Florida, Charisma House

Ref 10   Mark 14: 60. Ecclesia Bible Society. 2012. *The Voice Bible: Step into the Story of Scripture.* Nashville: Thomas Nelson.

Ref 11   Psalm 1. Ecclesia Bible Society. 2012. *The Voice Bible: Step into the Story of Scripture.* Nashville: Thomas Nelson.

Ref 12   Grenz, Stanley J, Jay T. Smith. 2015. *Created For Community: Connecting Christian Belief with Christian Living.* Baker Academic. Grand Rapids: Mi.

CHAPTER SIXTEEN

A Convincing Sound

'We are all broken and wounded in this world. Some choose to grow strong at the broken places' [1]
HAROLD J. DUARTE-BERNHARDT

A hunter needs to do his homework if he wants to imitate the bugle sounds of a bull elk. The range of vocal sounds are different and each one has a unique sound that communicates different things to the herd. From chuckles to glunking, right down to warning barks,[2] hunter's need to make certain that their bugling calls are accurate if they are going to persuade a bull elk to investigate the sound, causing him to move away from the herd. However, regardless of how convincing a hunter's bugle call sounds are, some bull elks will not move away from the herd. If he's an old bull elk, then he's managed to survive for as long as he has by learning from his past experiences. His judgment in listening out for fake sounds, possibly cultivated from a few scars that tell the stories of a couple of close encounters he's had with a hunter wanting to mount his magnificent head on his trophy wall, has caused the old bull to grow strong-willed, knowing his foe and distinguishing the sound from a truthful call to a counterfeit call that always gives away the hunter's fake, bogus cries.

The Belt of Truth

Knowing the truthful sound of authentic bugle calls helps us in the longevity of our faith and keep us moving forward toward our calling. Dead-ends and detours can leave us confused and susceptible to the fake bugle calls from the hunter, Satan which only leads to more wounding. The belt is a central part of the armour and when we buckle truth around our waists we will hear the legitimate sound of Jesus – the One who calls out to us even when we try to hide from Him. As I mentioned previously, I ran for many years because of fake bugle calls, and it took humility and trust before I decided to be brave enough to come out of hiding and repent for my actions, allowing myself to listen to the convincing sound of truth my ears had long forgotten that helped me find the path of the blood trail that led me back to Jesus. Perhaps like me,

Dead-ends and detours can leave us confused and susceptible to the fake bugle calls from the hunter, Satan which only leads to more wounding.

you've never really understood how to use the Belt of Truth that helps you to stop falling for the fake bugle calls of the hunter, Satan? Impostors have left you wounded and, on the run, leaving you humiliated rather than humble to know the truth of God's Word. Peter warns of false teachers in 2 Peter 2:2-3 because they give truth a bad name. They are only out for themselves.[3] We can be so badly wounded in our faith that it causes us to run and hide, making us afraid to become vulnerable again. However, the Belt of Truth can help us to recognise fake calls from the hunter, Satan straight away and tune into the authentic call of Jesus.

Hear My Voice

In John chapter 8, the new Jewish believers struggled to hear the accuracy of the call when Jesus teaches them 'If you hear my voice and abide in My word, you are truly My disciples, you will know the truth, and that truth will give you freedom.'[4] This statement gained the attention of a corrupt group who was plotting with the Romans to have Jesus crucified. Knowing this, Jesus turns His argument toward them. 'I come from the one True God, and I'm not here on My own. He sent Me on a mission. If God were your Father, you would know that and would love Me. You don't even understand what I'm saying. Do you? Why not? It is because you cannot stand to hear My voice. You are just like your true father, the devil; and you spend your time pursuing the things your father loves. He started out as a killer, and he cannot tolerate truth because he is void of anything true. At the core of his character, he is a liar; everything he speaks originates in these lies because he is the father of lies. So, when I speak truth, you don't believe Me.'[5]

The Belt of Truth responds to the sound of faith.

The Belt of Truth responds to the sound of our faith. Peter teaches us to gird up the loins of our minds, preparing us to be sober and rest our hope fully upon the grace that is to be brought to you by the revelation of Jesus Christ.⁶ This is where our strength to resist fake bugle calls comes from.

What Is Truth?

When Jesus was brought to the Praetorium which was the palace of Pontius Pilate⁷ in John chapter 19, Pilate asks Jesus 'Are you a king then?' Because of Jesus' reference to a kingdom that was not of this world, Pilate was intrigued by Jesus. Jesus stands firm and directly answers Pilate saying 'You say rightly that I am king. For this cause I was born, and for this cause I have come into this world, that I should bear witness to the truth. Everyone who is of the truth hears My voice.' Pilate said to Him, 'What is truth?' And when he had said this, he went out again to the Jews, and said to them, 'I find no fault in him at all.' ⁸

Pilate, an intelligent, cultured Roman may have understood Jesus as a philosopher as they described themselves as ideal rulers and claimed to be the only true kings, so Pilate would have probably seen Jesus as innocent.⁹ However, He was falsely accused and found 'guilty' of blasphemy and did go to the cross, sacrificing Himself so we could know the truth, and the Belt of Truth was used in the

When Jesus died, the bugle call of truth still sounded out to people.

chapter leading to Jesus' crucifixion. Finally, when Jesus died, the bugle call of truth still sounded out to people. 'So, when the centurion and those with him, who were guarding Jesus, saw the earthquake and the things that had happened, they feared greatly, saying, 'Truly this was the Son of God!'[10]

The truth of God's Word keeps us out of the thicket and on the right path. Psalm 25:4-5 reminds us to 'Show me Your ways, O Lord; teach me Your paths. Lead me in Your truth and teach me, for You are the God of my salvation; on You I wait all the day'[11] Following fake bugle calls rather than the authentic call of Jesus lands us in trouble and the hunter, Satan will steer you toward a dark and lonely path so he can wound you to start a blood trail. 1 John 1:5-10 lights up the path we are to follow, the path that is sprinkled with the redemptive blood Jesus left for us at the cross. 'This is the message we have heard from Him and declare to you: God is light; in Him there is no darkness at all. If we claim to have fellowship with Him yet walk in the darkness, we lie and do not live by the truth. But if we walk in the light, as He is in the light, we have fellowship with one another, and the blood of Jesus, His Son, purifies us from all sin.'[12] Gird your waist with the Belt of Truth, dear friend, and you will recognise fake bugle calls from the hunter, Satan in an instant. Walk in the light of God's truth and follow the illuminated path that reveals the redemption blood trail of Jesus. Let Him heal your wounds and lead you to the convincing sound of His truth.

> **Walk in the light of God's truth and follow the illuminated path that reveals the redemption blood trail of Jesus.**

Endnotes: Chapter Sixteen

Ref 1   Quotes. Pinterest.

Ref 2   elkhuntersguide.com/home/elk-sounds-2/

Ref 3   2 Peter 2:2-3 Peterson, Eugene H. 2000. *The Message Bible:* Colorado Springs, Colorado. Navpress.

Ref 4   John 8:31 Ecclesia Bible Society. 2012. *The Voice Bible: Step into the Story of Scripture.* Nashville: Thomas Nelson.

Ref 5   John 8:42-45 Ecclesia Bible Society. 2012. *The Voice Bible: Step into the Story of Scripture.* Nashville: Thomas Nelson.

Ref 6   1 Peter 1:13 *Spiritual Warfare Bible, NKJV.* 2012. Lake Mary, Florida, Charisma House

Ref 7   Praetorium – Wikipedia

Ref 8   John19:37-38 *Spiritual Warfare Bible, NKJV.* 2012. Lake Mary, Florida, Charisma House

Ref 9   Keener, Craig S. 1993. *The IVP Bible Background Commentary: New Testament.* Downers Grove, Ill. InterVarsity Press.

Ref 10   Matthew 27:54 *Spiritual Warfare Bible, NKJV.* 2012. Lake Mary, Florida, Charisma House

Ref 11   Psalm 25:4-5 *Spiritual Warfare Bible, NKJV.* 2012. Lake Mary, Florida, Charisma House

Ref 12   1 John 1:5-10. Syswerda, Jean, and Faith Organization. 2001. *NIV Women of Faith Study Bible: New International Version.* Grand Rapids, Mich.: Zondervan.

CHAPTER SEVENTEEN

Best Defence

'One has to be wounded in order to become a healer' [1]
MARIE LOUISE VON FRANZ

Bull elks understand they have a reputation to protect, and any sign of weakness must be hidden and covered up by the male if they want a harem of cows to trust them enough to mate with during the rutting season. Sparing is where males will fight with one another using their antlers as weapons to show which one is the most dominant. The elk's antler's main purposes are for defence and protection. The Breastplate of Righteousness is the piece of armour which protects and defends our heart. So, what is righteousness exactly? Other words are; uprightness, virtue, respectability.[2] All noble words, however, this is where things can get a little tricky because we need to understand how to use the Breastplate well so the hunter, Satan doesn't turn this weapon against us.

If we start fashioning our own breastplate so it covers our reputations instead of our hearts, then we'll lead from our own strength and strive from our own form of righteousness that only leads to more wounding. My church experiences have left their scars, and I'm glad. They remind me that I need to constantly wear the Breastplate of Jesus' Righteousness and not the one I've formed and fashioned myself to impress God and others. If I'm to continue to lead from a healthy heart and not an emotionally damaged heart,[3] then these hard-won truths from my past reveal what happens when you choose to protect your reputation rather than reflect truth and holiness that only comes from Jesus' righteousness. And for this reason, I want especially for you, dear friend, to use this piece of armour well.

A Heart Shot isn't to Wound

'Character refers to who you are. Reputation refers to who people think you are'[4] reminds Emily P. Freeman. The hunter, Satan has used this against me so the Breastplate of Righteousness hangs low and I'm vulnerable for his attack. A heart shot isn't to wound and blood trail you by the hunter. Oh no, this shot is fatal, and that is why it's so vitally important we know Who's righteousness is doing all the covering. As believers, to make sure the Breastplate is a good fit over our hearts we need to keep to the long and winding path that is paved with truth and holiness, otherwise we will undo ourselves if we try to find a quicker way.[5] I've

> **It's so vitally important we know Who's righteousness is doing all the covering.**

talked about being under the authority of a pastor who protected his charismatic reputation more than walking the path of truth and holiness in a previous chapter. Sadly, this allowed his self-serving motives to go unnoticed, and sadder still, I have to admit, that his charismatic personality over his character, and to add to that, the title and position I held, only fuelled my performance-based mindset which caused me to never develop enough courage or confidence to confront certain things that would have possibly resulted in my own reputation coming under scrutiny.

Paul reminds us in 2 Corinthians 5:20 that we are ambassadors for Christ, 'representatives of the Liberating King.'[6] Reconciliation means Jesus agreed to pay for all our sins once and for all, 'the Anointed One, who never experienced sin, became sin for us so that in Him we might embody the very righteousness of God'[4] When charisma becomes the magnet that draws us away from the character of a person it can set us up for further wounding because inevitably, they're going to let us down. Knowing this hard-won truth has made me a better, more confident leader because I've learned to look for character rather than becoming mesmerized by charisma.

> When charisma becomes the magnet that draws us away from the character of a person it can set us up for further wounding because inevitably, they're going to let us down.

A Gap to Shoot an Arrow

Whenever Jesus had an encounter with the Pharisees, He'd expose their motives and arrogance behind their do-it-yourself breastplates. 'Woe to you, [self-righteous] scribes and Pharisees, hypocrites! For you clean the outside of the cup and of the plate, but inside they are full of extortion and robbery and self-indulgence [unrestrained greed]. You [spiritually] blind Pharisee, first clean the inside of the cup and of the plate [examine and change your inner self to conform to God's precepts], so that the outside [your public life and deeds] may be clean also.[7] Jesus was warning the Pharisees that they were serving out of their self-righteousness, even though everyone thought highly of this group of believers and believed that they were God's elite representatives.[8] However, they were reflecting their own standards on their breastplates which only mirrored their self-important, egotistical attitudes that Jesus came to change.

The deep-seated, rooted sin in our hearts means that each and every one of us fall short of God's standard[9] and this is why Paul knew we needed the Breastplate of Righteousness in our armoury, so we keep walking step by step along the truth and holiness path. Remember, the weapons of the war we're fighting are not of this world but are powered by God and effective at tearing down the strongholds erected against His

Strongholds, if not dealt with, can be the undoing of a believer, so it's so important to guard our heart with the Breastplate God offers us against the hunter, Satan's arrows.

truth.[10] Strongholds, if not dealt with, can be the undoing of a believer, so it's so important to guard our heart with the Breastplate God offers us against the hunter, Satan's arrows. When our reputation comes under fire, it will be our character that pulls us through. It doesn't matter how spiritual we believe we are, if what we say and what we do don't match up then we have no business becoming the hypocritical dishwashing Pharisee to other people's 'cups and plates'. I'm not saying we have to be perfect; this is the reason why we so desperately need the real Breastplate of Righteousness of Jesus rather than the one we manufacture for ourselves. None of us measure up to the high standards of God. But if the hunter, Satan can find the tiniest crack in your makeshift breastplate which was stitched together by what others think of you and polished with your charisma, you can guarantee he'll find that gap and shoot his arrow straight into the heart of your character before you've even had time to know what hit you.

He'll find that gap and shoot his arrow straight into the heart of your character before you've even had time to know what hit you.

No Reputation

The hunter doesn't care about the reputation of a bull elk, he just wants to wound the elk so he can start a blood trail that hopefully ends with the elk's weapons (his antlers) mounted on his trophy wall. And just like the elk's best defence weapon, homemade breastplates will be rendered useless against the wiles of our enemy if we don't learn to strap on the true Breastplate of Righteousness and live out our faith with integrity in truth and holiness. The wonderful character trait of Jesus, is that He made Himself of no reputation, taking the form of a bondservant... humbling Himself and became obedient to the point of death, even death on a cross.[11] So why do we cling to our reputations so tightly if Jesus made sure He had no reputation? Isaiah 53:3 paints a picture of how unimportant reputation was to Jesus because He had no beauty or majesty to attract us to him, nothing in his appearance that we should desire him. He was despised and rejected by men, a man of sorrows, and familiar with suffering. Like one from whom men hide their faces, he was despised, and we esteemed him not.[12] No charisma, just a solid character that came from walking in truth and holiness. Every privilege that His status could have clung to, He gave up, and because of that obedience, God lifted Jesus up and honoured Him far beyond anyone or anything.[13] The Pharisees corrected people with their rules and reputations, but Jesus rescued and redeemed sinners back to God by giving them the Breastplate of His Righteousness so the gaping hole in the relationship between Himself and man was closed.

> **Why do we cling to our reputations so tightly if Jesus made sure He had no reputation?**

Amazing Grace

The amazing grace of Jesus was never more astonishing than in His last few moments as He slowly died on the cross. Even though

His flesh was hanging by the nails that held His bloodied hands and feet in place, He still showed the wounded the way home. 'Jesus wasn't the only one being crucified that day. There were two others, criminals, who were also being led to their execution.[14] Joining in with the soldiers mocking, one of the criminals said to Jesus, 'You're supposed to be the Anointed One, right? Well – do it! Rescue Yourself and us! But the other criminal told him to be quiet. 'Don't you have any fear of God at all? You're getting the same death sentence He is! We're getting what we deserve since we've committed crimes, but this man hasn't done anything wrong at all! (turning to Jesus) 'Jesus, when You come into Your kingdom, please remember me.' 'I promise you that this very day you will be with Me in paradise.'[15] The Pharisees required rules, Jesus required relationship.

> **He still showed the wounded the way home.**

Jesus' death created a path for our rescue and reconciliation, for the salvation of our wounded souls regardless of our reputations. A blood trail for us to follow that we truly didn't deserve.

Endnotes: Chapter Seventeen

Ref 1   Quotes Pinterest.

Ref 2   thesaurus. com

Ref 3   Scazzero, Peter. 2015. *Emotionally Healthy Leader – How Transforming Your Inner Life Will Deeply T.* Zondervan.

Ref 4   Freeman, Emily P. 2011. *Grace for the Good Girl: Letting Go of the Try-Hard Life.* Published by Revell, Baker publishing Group .. Grand Rapids. Mi. USA.

Ref 5   Gurnall, William. 2010. *The Christian in Complete Armour.* Peabody, Mass.: Hendrickson ; Edinburgh.

Ref 6   2 Corinthians 5:20 Ecclesia Bible Society. 2012. *The Voice Bible: Step into the Story of Scripture.* Nashville: Thomas Nelson.

Ref 7   Matthew 23:25-26 *Amplified Holy Bible : Compact : Captures the Full Meaning behind the Original Greek and Hebrew.* 2015. Grand Rapids, Michigan: Zondervan.

Ref 8   Osborne, Larry W. 2012. *Accidental Pharisees: Avoiding Pride, Exclusivity, and other Dangers of Overzealous Faith.* Grand Rapids, Mich.: Zondervan.

Ref 9   Created For Community Stanley Grenz and Jay Smith page 61 'Our Human Failure'

Ref 10   2 Corinthians 10:4 Ecclesia Bible Society. 2012. *The Voice Bible: Step into the Story of Scripture.* Nashville: Thomas Nelson.

Ref 11   Philippians 2:7-8 *Spiritual Warfare Bible, NKJV.* 2012. Lake Mary, Florida, Charisma House

Ref 12   Isaiah 53:3 Syswerda, Jean, and Faith Organization. 2001. *NIV Women of Faith Study Bible: New International Version.* Grand Rapids, Mich.: Zondervan.

Ref 13   Philippians 2:5-11 Peterson, Eugene H. 2000. *The Message Bible:* Colorado Springs, Colorado. Navpress.

Ref 14   Luke 23:32 Ecclesia Bible Society. 2012. *The Voice Bible: Step into the Story of Scripture.* Nashville: Thomas Nelson.

Ref 15   Luke 23:39-43 Ecclesia Bible Society. 2012. *The Voice Bible: Step into the Story of Scripture.* Nashville: Thomas Nelson.

CHAPTER EIGHTEEN

Fancy Footwork

'Her ways are pleasant ways, and all her paths are peace.'[1]
PROVERBS 3:17

Did you know that an elk's anklebones make a distinct sound when they walk? This fancy footwork is the primary means of communication and engagement with others. As their ankles crack and pop, it's believed that this sound is one elk communicating to other elks that their approaching from behind them.[2] I've had the privilege of being in church leadership for almost twenty years, and during that time my ears have become tuned to the distinct sounds of dysfunctional leadership and the poor communication which bad leadership brings. Unfortunately, if we don't make good communication a priority, then this neglect will only lead to more hurts and wounds within the church. Rather than hearing an elk within your herd approaching from behind you, it will be the hunter, Satan who wants to wound you badly, starting a blood trail that can keep you running for years.

Jesus made it a priority to communicate with His disciples during his three-year ministry. His fancy footwork made the distinct sound of good mentorship as He took the time to explain and show His disciples the culture of God's kingdom. Not only did this encourage growth in the disciple's faith, but it also built trust within the group. Jesus asked the disciples questions, drawing out their own beliefs, misconceptions, and worldviews. He helped the visual learners with parables and stories that cut through the noise of confusion, leaving His disciples slack-jawed and full of more questions that went to the heart of each issue they faced internally. He built up His disciple's confidence over His three-year ministry and helped them understand important truths and values of God's upside-down kingdom. Why? Because they had to listen out for unfamiliar sounds.

Be Alert!

Jesus needed His disciples to know the 'sounds' of the hunter, Satan, and be alert at all times. These sounds can be difficult to distinguish at first, however, the more you become accustomed to the Voice of the Good Shepherd, the more you'll recognise the hunter's strange sounds that never bellow out offence, bitterness, rivalry, or compromise. No, these sounds only come in whispers and murmurs from behind you, that poke, prod and question the

> **Jesus needed His disciples to know the 'sounds' of the hunter, Satan, and be alert at all times.**

unprotected areas of your faith. Ephesians 4:27 reminds us to not give the devil a foothold. This means we should never give him space to move in close and to pull back his bow and let the poison-tipped arrow go straight into our thinking. If unfamiliar sounds can sprinkle a little suspicion within the herd, then it's game over, and the hunter, Satan will have a leader's head mounted on his heavily decorated trophy wall quicker than you can say, 'what's that noise?' I've seen leaders fall because they've not paid attention to the ambush of the hunter, and believe me when I tell you, it's devastating to watch. But how do we stop poor communication becoming an offence, leaving us wounded and on the run?

Shoes of the Gospel of Peace

The shoes of the Gospel of Peace is the fourth piece of armour we need, which helps steady our feet in our Christian walk and it's possibly the most important. When soldiers advanced toward the enemy in battle, they couldn't afford to lose their concentration in worrying about stepping on something.[3] In the Old Testament, if you were in the infantry of the Assyrian army, it was common to go into battle barefooted because only the cavalry were equipped with knee-high boots, making the shoes valuable items to plunder from the slain soliders.[4] Good

Good communication which builds strong connection with each other and with God, stops the hunter, Satan from plundering our shoes of peace.

communication which builds strong connection with each other and with God, stops the hunter, Satan from plundering our shoes of peace. 'I have told you these things, so that in me you may have peace. In this world you will have trouble. But take heart! I have overcome the world' [5] reminds Jesus, right before His arrest in the Garden of Gethsemane. Another translation says, 'And everything I've taught you is so that the peace which is in me will be in you and give you great confidence as you rest in me.'[6] The calm in Jesus was going to help sustain Him through the storm leading toward the cross, and He was communicating to His disciples that His peace was where they were going to find great confidence when they decided to run away and hide because of fear.

The shoes of the Gospel of Peace Jesus wore at His trial in John chapter eighteen, communicated to Pilate that He had done nothing wrong. 'He's not guilty. I couldn't find one fault with him. Now you know that we have a custom that I release one prisoner every year at Passover – shall I release your king – the king of the Jews?' asks Pilate, hoping to be done with the matter. But the crowd shouted over and over, 'No, not him! Give us Barabbas!' [7]

> **The calm in Jesus was going to help sustain Him through the storm leading toward the cross.**

Barabbas was guilty. This troublemaking zealot whose fancy footwork in leading a rebellion wasn't going to go unpunished as far as the Romans were concerned. Nevertheless, none of that swayed the crowd and instead they released a criminal and condemned an innocent person to death. The one who had led an insurrection was now being freed because of the

One who leads the resurrection. Barabbas was the leader of a rebellion and became the image of every son of Adam who had rebelled against God. [8] Jesus stood firm in His shoes of Peace over the difficulty and danger of what was about to happen. And as the distinct sounds of the cracks and pops rang out, they communicated that a path was being paved toward our deliverance and freedom.

Run Toward the Melody

Our wounds reveal that in this world we do indeed experience trouble and times of testing. However, we have a choice to either listen to the unfamiliar 'sounds' of the hunter, Satan, or do we put our elk hooves into the shoes that bring Peace and run toward its melody? Jesus offers us the Peace which is in Him so it will be in you and give you great confidence. Resting in Him means we don't allow offence, bitterness, rivalry, or compromise to shake His Peace that is within us. Mistrust becomes unbelief which leads to rebellion. Don't make the same mistake the Israelites did when they allowed their difficult desert experiences to question their faith in God. 'Today, if you hear his voice, do not harden your hearts as you did in the rebellion.' Who were they who heard and rebelled? Were they not all those Moses led out of Egypt? [9]

> **Do we put our elk hooves into the shoes that bring Peace and run toward its melody?**

We need to support each other in good communication and be the peacemakers rather than the troublemakers, a herd of believers that huddle together during hunting season. Wearing the shoes that bring His Peace gives our hooved feet strength because there is strength in numbers. An insecure, unsteady elk is more easily picked off by the hunter than a whole herd who is sure-footed in the faith. Wounded ones who have lost their peace will see His peace within you and wonder where your sure-footed faith comes from. You can tell them that it comes from 'The True God who encircled me with strength and made my pathway straight. He made me sure-footed as a deer and placed me high up where I am safe...You taught me how to walk with care so my feet will not slip.' [10] The Israelites faced trials and tests in the desert, and they failed to trust that God had the victory. They trusted in themselves and ran.[11] Having the sure-footed, sense of peace faith in knowing that deliverance and freedom comes even through our troubles and difficulties. When our circumstances seem most desperate this is where the shoes of the Gospel of Peace lift and help us to step up into the higher, rugged terrain where the hunter, Satan won't be able to find us so easily.

> An insecure, unsteady elk is more easily picked off by the hunter than a whole herd who is sure-footed in the faith.

Endnotes: Chapter Eighteen

Ref 1   Quote - Proverbs 3:17 Syswerda, Jean, and Faith Organization. 2001. *NIV Women of Faith Study Bible: New International Version.* Grand Rapids, Mich.: Zondervan.

Ref 2   8 Fascinating facts about Elk by Tyler Wilcox. May 06, 2019. Article.

Ref 3   Keener, Craig S. 1993. *The IVP Bible Background Commentary: New Testament.* Downers Grove, Ill. InterVarsity Press.

Ref 4   Walton, John H, Victor Harold Matthew, and Mark William Chavalas. 2000. *The IVP Bible Background Commentary: Old Testament.* Downers Grove, Ill. InterVarsity Press.

Ref 5   John 16:33 Syswerda, Jean, and Faith Organization. 2001. *NIV Women of Faith Study Bible: New International Version.* Grand Rapids, Mich.: Zondervan.

Ref 6   John 16:33 *The Passion Translation: New Testament with Psalms, Proverbs, and Song of Songs, Second Edition.* Passion & Fire Ministries, Inc. BroadStreet Publishing: 2018.

Ref 7   John 18: 38-40 *The Passion Translation: New Testament with Psalms, Proverbs, and Song of Songs, Second Edition.* Passion & Fire Ministries, Inc. BroadStreet Publishing: 2018.

Ref 8   Commentary on page 297 *The Passion Translation: New Testament with Psalms, Proverbs, and Song of Songs, Second Edition.* Passion & Fire Ministries, Inc. BroadStreet Publishing: 2018.

Ref 9   Hebrews 3:15-16 Syswerda, Jean, and Faith Organization. 2001. *NIV Women of Faith Study Bible: New International Version.* Grand Rapids, Mich.: Zondervan.

Ref 10   Psalm 19:32-36 Ecclesia Bible Society. 2012. *The Voice Bible: Step into the Story of Scripture.* Nashville: Thomas Nelson.

Ref 11   Commentary 'Trusting when Tested.' Syswerda, Jean, and Faith Organization. 2001. *NIV Women of Faith Study Bible: New International Version.* Grand Rapids, Mich.: Zondervan.

CHAPTER NINETEEN

Firing Arrows

*'It's not out of the heart that people do damaging things.
Rather, it's out of the wounds of the heart.'* [1]
CRAIG D. LOUNSBROUGH

Bull elks are very protective of their harem during the rut and will fight other male elks and intruders who try to steal their cows. These fights can become very intense as the bull elk defends his territory and his harem of vulnerable cows with every ounce of courage and strength he can muster, shielding his herd so fiercely that it can sometimes lead to his death.

Bull elks protect the mothers of their calves and in His final moments, Jesus made sure His mother would be shielded and protected after His death. Mary lived in a culture where women did not earn a great deal of income, so the mother would depend on her eldest son for financial support. [2] And with many bulls surrounding Jesus, raging, and roaring at Him ³ as He hung on the cross, He shielded His herd with what little strength He had left.

Looking back on my years of the hunter, Satan blood trailing me, I realise now that there were crucial moments in my leadership where the impulse to run away because of my inward pain outweighed the need to protect and shield others from the arrows and bullets of the hunter, sending other believers on their own blood trail. The hunter's arrows had left festering wounds of distrust and offence that rocked my once firm, stable faith causing the Shield of Faith to lay on the forest floor. The hunter, Satan knows that the wounds of offence can keep us focused on ourselves, causing us to run and isolate from the community of believers.

> **The hunter, Satan knows that the wounds of offence can keep us focused on ourselves, causing us to run and isolate from the community of believers.**

I find it interesting how only four people stood by the cross in Jesus' last moments. Where were the multitudes of people Jesus had healed of their diseases, in Luke 6:17? Or the five thousand Jesus had fed with a boy's lunch in Matthew chapter 14? Even eleven of the Twelve had deserted Him, abandoning their faith because of shame, fear, and anguish that their Saviour, their rescuer, the One who's kingdom was coming now hung wounded and dying on a wooden cross.

I have no cause to judge them, I too abandoned Him when I failed to take up the Shield, leaving my faith wide open for the hunter's fiery arrows to pierce my faith. 'Don't you feel my pain?' we cry as we try to patch up our swollen, infected wounds that have left a blood trail for the hunter, Satan to follow. And as we pull out the arrowheads of accusation and blame, we aim them back at the community of believers, the church who let us down in our faith, the leaders who said they would cover us, shield us from hurt, protect us from further wounding by the hunter.

The writer of Hebrews speaks a lot about faith. 'Let us hold fast the confession of our hope without wavering, for He who promised is faithful' (Heb10:23) 'Therefore do not cast away your confidence, which has great reward. For you have need of endurance, so that after you have done the will of God, you may receive the promise...now the just shall live by faith; but if anyone draws back, my soul has no pleasure in him' (Heb 10:35-38) 'Now faith is the substance of things hoped for, for the evidence of things not seen.' (Heb 11:1) '...let us run with endurance the race that is set before us, looking unto Jesus the author and finisher of our faith, who for the joy that was set before Him endured the cross, despising the shame, and has sat down at the right hand of the throne of God' (Heb 12:2) [4]

It seems the Hebrews writer uses the word endurance a lot whenever he's talking about faith, and as Jesus' life slowly slipped away, He knew, as a leader, He needed to equip and help others gain the grit, fortitude, and courage to keep going in their faith when things got tough. The hunter, Satan wounds us with his accusing arrows and bombards us

> **The hunter, Satan wounds us with his accusing arrows and bombards us with bullets from his rifle to break our trust with God.**

with bullets from his rifle to break our trust with God, and in turn, we do his dirty work for him by turning the arrows of blame and shame on the body of believers. I have learned the painful and hard way to carry my Shield of Faith at all times, regardless of how many arrows the hunter shoots at me because the people I lead need my protection, they need me to shield them from the hunter, and like the bull elk, I will fight for the herd.

I want to you to know the secret as to why the hunter, Satan doesn't want you to carry your Shield of Faith well. It is because, 'A [Spartan] warrior carries helmet and breastplate for his own protection, but his shield for the safely of the whole line.'⁵ Our responsibility as believers, and more so for leaders, is to look out for the whole line. The Shield reflects your trust in Jesus and the hope that He, and He alone, will turn your wounds into victorious scars. When Jesus predicted Peter's denial in Luke 22:32, He tells Peter He has prayed for him that his faith should not fail, '...I have prayed that your faith will hold firm and that you will recover from your failure and become a source of strength for your brothers here.'⁶ Peter, perceived leader of the disciples, denied that he would abandon his faith, however, he did, and Jesus restored him so he could gain the strength and courage to carry the Shield to help others in the faith.

> **The Shield reflects your trust in Jesus and the hope that He, and He alone, will turn your wounds into victorious scars.**

Like Peter, our wounding has caused us to not trust Jesus completely, and wounded elks have a habit of running when things get tough making us drop the Shield all too quickly. Even though Jesus knew He'd be betrayed, let down, and abandoned, He helped renew and restore the disciples after His resurrection. But it was too late for one disciple, Judas. He allowed his selfishness to dump the Shield of Faith so his hands could be free to grab the thirty pieces of silver that the Pharisees offered him, eventually leading Judas to be so wounded from remorse and regret that he took his own life. But 'the Spirit's intent in conviction, however, is not to cause our death but to foster eternal life. He desires that we not only see our sin but also turn to God for forgiveness and healing'. [7] Our Shield of Faith is for the covering of others, the protection of the herd. If we protect and cover our faith with the Shield and keep running toward the blood trail Jesus left behind at the cross, if we keep protecting our relationship with Jesus regardless of our circumstances and despite our wounding then it doesn't matter how many arrows or bullets the hunter, Satan shoots to try to penetrate our faith, the Shield of Faith is firmly in place because of our trust is in Jesus.

> Our Shield of Faith is for the covering of others, the protection of the herd.

Paul writes about his own wounds and pain, 'Praise be to the God and Father of our Lord Jesus Christ, the Father of compassion and the God of all comfort, who comforts us in all our troubles, so that we can comfort those in any trouble with the comfort we ourselves have received from God. For just as the sufferings of Christ flow over into our lives, so also through Christ our comfort overflows.'[8] Jesus showed us patient endurance through His pain and suffering on the cross so that we could take hold of the Shield of Faith to help, encourage, and protect others in the faith, and to give us the strength so we are able to run with courageous persistence.

Endnotes: Chapter Nineteen

Ref 1 Quotes Pinterest

Ref 2 Keener, Craig S. 1993. *The IVP Bible Background Commentary: New Testament.* Downers Grove, Ill. InterVarsity Press.

Ref 3 Psalm 22:12 *Spiritual Warfare Bible, NKJV.* 2012. Lake Mary, Florida, Charisma House

Ref 4 (Heb10:23) (Heb 10:35-38) (Heb 11:1) (Heb 12:2) *Spiritual Warfare Bible, NKJV.* 2012. Lake Mary, Florida, Charisma House

Ref 5 Sinek, Simon. 2019. *Leaders Eat Last: Why Some Teams Pull Together and Others Don't.* London. United Kingdom. Penguin Random House.

Ref 6 Luke 22:32.Ecclesia Bible Society. 2012. *The Voice Bible: Step into the Story of Scripture.* Nashville: Thomas Nelson.

Ref 7 Stanley J, Jay T. Smith. 2015. *Created For Community: Connecting Christian Belief with Christian Living.* Baker Academic. Grand Rapids: Mi.

Ref 8 2 Corinthians 1:3-5 Syswerda, Jean, and Faith Organization. 2001. *NIV Women of Faith Study Bible: New International Version.* Grand Rapids, Mich.: Zondervan.

CHAPTER TWENTY

Level of Pressure

'Within Your wounds, hide me!' [1]
EVELYN UNDERHILL

Given there are many hunters around in the hunting season, the human scent is more prevalent than other animals. Elk are big game animals, and their sense of smell is highly capable of sniffing out an amateur hunter. So, the pressure is on for an experienced hunter to be more rigorous in eliminating his scent while tracking an elk. Staying scent free is pivotal if a hunter wants to go home with some venison. However, unlike the hunter, we cannot stay scent free if we are to keep from being blood trailed. Becoming diligent and immersing ourselves in God's Word is what's going to cover us in an odour which is going to protect us from being hunted. When Satan takes one whiff, he will recognise it and find it a very distasteful and repugnant smell, causing him to retreat.

Elks have a recognisable smell. Their livestock-like scent has sour, musky overtones and can linger in the area they've been in for a few days.[2] Believers have a recognisable smell too. In 2 Corinthians 2:14-15 the scent is 'Through our yielded lives he spreads his fragrance of the knowledge of God everywhere we go. We have become the unmistakable aroma of the victory of the Anointed One to God – a perfume of life to those being saved and the odour of death to those who are perishing.'[3] When the hunter, Satan finds areas we've been in, it is Jesus' scent that lingers. Satan recognises it straight away because it is the smell of victory. That distasteful stench which forces him to remember his failure at the cross. It lingers over him. That triumphant aroma which concluded his defeat once and for all, lingers. It lingers when we put God's law in our hearts and write them upon our minds.[4] (Hebrews 10:16)

> When the hunter, Satan finds areas we've been in, it is Jesus' scent that lingers.

Sword of the Spirit

The Sword of the Spirit is a solid piece of the armour we need to protect ourselves with. It is the logos, the rhema, the double-edged sword of the Spirit that ties the hands of the hunter so he cannot reach for his weapon.

'In the beginning was the Word, and the Word was with God, and the Word was God. He was with God in the beginning'[5] states John at the start of his gospel account. When we face pressure from the hunter, Satan and catch his repugnant scent, we can use the double-edged sword to protect us. In Matthew chapter four, we read about the temptation of Jesus. Each temptation Satan questions the identity and authority of Jesus. However, the hunter overplayed his hand, and his excessive confidence and mistaken optimism was confronted by the incense of the Word. Jesus didn't just use the Sword of the Spirit when He was questioned by Satan, He *was* the Sword. 'It is written...' was the moment Satan suddenly realised he'd brought a plastic gun to a double-edged knife fight.

When Satan challenges, questions, and pressures us, when he pokes at our identity and tests our authority we need to be adequately equipped and cover ourselves in the aroma of the Word so we can confidently walk through any traps he's set up. Psalm 91:14-15 says, 'Because you have delighted in me my great lover, I will greatly protect you. I will set you in a high place, safe and secure before my face. I will answer your cry for help every time you pray, and you will find and feel my presence even in your time of pressure and trouble.' [6]

The beauty of the Sword of the Spirit is that it's double-edged. A weapon that is both defensive and offensive.[7] Revelation 12:11 claims the finished work of Jesus at the cross, 'They overcame him by

> The testimony of our scars tell people our stories.

the blood of the Lamb and by the word of their testimony.' And the testimony of our scars tell people our stories. Powerful reminders that God is always moulding, shaping, and forging our attitudes, our posture, and our hearts with the Sword of the Spirit so we can handle it well.

A few years ago, when my friend was helping me process some of the setbacks and disappointments during the church plant fail which had caused deep wounding, she said to me, 'You smell of battle.' Clearly, I had gained a recognisable smell that the hunter, Satan didn't like, and I believe that the aroma came because I made sure reading and using my Bible became an important part of my faith. If we're to stop the hunter, Satan from wounding us and stop him from starting a blood trail we need to recognise his odour. 'Stay alert.' Peter reminds us, 'The Devil is poised to pounce and would like nothing better than to catch you napping. Keep your guard up' [8] Elks need to stay vigilant during hunting season and we do too because our masquerade, performance-based, insincere religious activities have no power. We must soak ourselves in the unmistakable aroma of the victory found in the pages of His Word. I've come to realise that the aroma of religion stinks and has no room for authentic, vulnerable faith. It has no time for ugly tears and struggles, so you learn to just go through the motions which does nothing to stop the hunter from blood trailing you.

> Elks need to stay vigilant during hunting season and we do too because our masquerade, performance-based, insincere religious activities have no power.

The Sword of the Spirit builds a deep connection with Jesus, the One who endured the breaking so we could be made whole. The injuries that He suffered became our healing. [9]

This Inside-Out, Upside-Down King

'The governor's soldiers took Jesus into the great hall, gathered a great crowd, and stripped Jesus of His clothes, draping Him in a bold scarlet cloak, the kind the soldiers sometimes wore. They gathered some thorny vines, wove them into a crown, and perched that crown upon His head. They stuck a reed in His right hand, and then they knelt before Him, this inside-out, upside-down King. They mocked Him with catcalls. 'Hail, the King of the Jews.'[10] A deep connection with this inside-out, upside-down King causes us to smell of battle. A King who helps you to let go of everything that is surface-level and superficial in your faith, like a Black Friday sale, all religious stuff needs to go. Wounds can have an odour if not cleaned and bandaged and they can cause people to become cold and hard. But the more we read the story of the crucified Christ, the more we become thankful for His sacrifice on our behalf.

> **Like a Black Friday sale, all religious stuff needs to go.**

'Where is God in My Pain?'

'They spat on Him and whipped Him on the head with His sceptre of reeds, and when they had their fill, they pulled off the bold scarlet cloak, dressed Him in His own simple clothes, and led Him off to be crucified.'[11]

'Then they crucified Jesus, nailing his hands and feet to the cross.'[12]

Our wounds ask the question, 'Where is God in my pain?' And the sight and smell of Jesus' bruised, bloodied, and unrecognisable body which hung on that cross answers us. The Messiah, the Saviour, the Redeemer wasn't dressed in royal robes, wearing a gold crown, and riding a warhorse, ready to take on the Roman Empire as many had presumed. Instead, the Word had been spat on, whipped, and humiliated while wearing a soldier's scarlet cloak. His bloodied hair was wrapped around a crown made of thorns that mocked the very core of His identity and Kingship. 'Although He was a Son, Jesus learned obedience through the things He suffered. And once He was perfected through suffering, He became the way of salvation for all those who hear and follow Him.'[13] The version of a Saviour that the disciples longed for couldn't be formed because the clean shaven, cape wearing, squeaky clean Messiah they wanted would have no power or authority to heal every one of our wounds. The Word, in His suffering, had the strength in the breaking to overthrow Satan's rule. The endurance of the cross sealed our inheritance of eternal salvation. Religion says, 'I'm in charge' but obedience and self-sacrifice to an inside-out, upside-down King says, 'He's in charge.' The Sword of the Spirit pressures the hunter, Satan to retreat because it carries the recognisable aroma of sacrifice.

Endnotes: Chapter Twenty

Ref 1   (quote) Underhill, Evelyn, and Robyn Wrigley – Carr. 2018. *Evelyn Underhill's Prayer Book.* London: Spck Publishing.

Ref 2   krebscreek.com/what-do-elk-look-sound-and-smell-like (website)

Ref 3   2 Corinthians 2:14-15 *The Passion Translation: New Testament with Psalms, Proverbs, and Song of Songs, Second Edition.* Passion & Fire Ministries, Inc. BroadStreet Publishing: 2018.

Ref 4   Hebrews 10:16. Ecclesia Bible Society. 2012. *The Voice Bible: Step into the Story of Scripture.* Nashville: Thomas Nelson.

Ref 5   John 1:1-2 Syswerda, Jean, and Faith Organization. 2001. *NIV Women of Faith Study Bible: New International Version.* Grand Rapids, Mich.: Zondervan.

Ref 6   Psalm 91:14-15 *The Passion Translation: New Testament with Psalms, Proverbs, and Song of Songs, Second Edition.* Passion & Fire Ministries, Inc. BroadStreet Publishing: 2018.

Ref 7   Gurnall, William. 2010. *The Christian in Complete Armour.* Peabody, Mass.: Hendrickson ; Edinburgh.

Ref 8   1 Peter 5:8 Peterson, Eugene H. 2000. *The Message Bible:* Colorado Springs, Colorado. Navpress.

Ref 9   Isaiah 53:5 Ecclesia Bible Society. 2012. *The Voice Bible: Step into the Story of Scripture.* Nashville: Thomas Nelson.

Ref 10   Matthew 27:27-29 Ecclesia Bible Society. 2012. *The Voice Bible: Step into the Story of Scripture.* Nashville: Thomas Nelson.

Ref 11   Matthew 27:30-31 Ecclesia Bible Society. 2012. *The Voice Bible: Step into the Story of Scripture.* Nashville: Thomas Nelson.

Ref 12   Matthew 27:35 *The Passion Translation: New Testament with Psalms, Proverbs, and Song of Songs, Second Edition.* Passion & Fire Ministries, Inc. BroadStreet Publishing: 2018.

Ref 13   Hebrews 5:8-9 Ecclesia Bible Society. 2012. *The Voice Bible: Step into the Story of Scripture.* Nashville: Thomas Nelson.

CHAPTER TWENTY-ONE

An Invitation

'He calls the wounded to be world changers.'[1]
ANN VOSKAMP

Henrik Thurfjell, an ecologist from the University of Alberta wanted to find out, along with his colleagues, why cow elks lived longer than bull elks. After tracking 49 cows for six years with GPS, they discovered that female elk live in groups, so they are less likely to become a single target for a hunter. Another reason Thurfjell discovered why cows live more than fifteen years longer than bulls could be that cows seem to spend the majority of their time in rugged terrain during hunting season, making them difficult for a hunter to get a good shot. However, the most interesting discovery was from his findings was that he believed cows may have developed different strategies depending on the different types of weapons the hunters used.[2] It sounds slightly ridiculous to think that female elks are able to change their game plan to avoid being wounded by a hunter, however, the female elk's approach has practically made them bulletproof.³

Valuable Scars

As our time together in this cosy wooden cabin in the forest draws to its conclusion, I do hope and pray that everything I have shared has helped you to change your game plan so you can avoid being blood trailed by the hunter in the future. I know as I've shared my story of wounding and shown you my valuable scars, Jesus has poured olive oil onto your wounds and disinfected them with His wine, making sure they are bandaged to stop the bleeding.⁴

Now that you know how to use each piece of armour Jesus left at the cross, you've practically become bulletproof, and I know you'll use the armour each day to stop the hunter's arrows or bullets penetrating your soul, making blood trailing a thing that stays firmly in your past. Nevertheless, as you slowly unwrap the bandages and admire your valuable scars where wounds once bled out, you need to forgive yourself for all the mistakes you've made. Shame is powerful and sometimes it can be easier to forgive others before we can even think about forgiving ourselves. I know, because when I think about my past, I struggle from time to time with the 'what if's' and the 'maybe if I'd have done that' moments that the hunter, Satan tries to pick at. But we cannot change our past, we can only look toward a better future.

Fully Healed. Fully Whole.

If there is one thing that I want to applaud you for, dear friend, it is the fact that you stayed and didn't run when you felt the sting of the disinfectant as Jesus poured His wine into your oozing, scabby wounds. You didn't bolt when the Apostle Paul trained you in the weapons of warfare to protect you from the hunter, Satan's shots. You allowed every heartbreak, every disappointment, and all the shame that surrounded those wounds to be fully healed so you became fully whole. You chose the higher ground over hiding as you ran along the path rather than running away, choosing to follow the blood trail of Jesus instead of leaving a blood trail behind you. Now you know nothing Satan can do could separate you from the love of Christ. No trouble or hardship or persecution or famine or nakedness or danger or sword…no, in all these things we are more than conquerors through Him who loved us.[5]

Sadly, many others still choose hiding over freedom by not surrendering and deciding to become as brave and courageous as you have, dear friend. Many still run as the blood trail from their wounding follows behind them because they believe they can outrun or outsmart the hunter.

> **Many still run as the blood trail from their wounding follows behind them because they believe they can outrun or outsmart the hunter.**

However, the hunter is very patient and eventually, over time he will take them down and mount their heads on his trophy wall. And it is this thought that I wrestle with, as it stirs me and leads me to action. It causes me to pray and to intercede for the wounded ones who still long for a place to rest their weary souls and let Jesus take care of their bleeding wounds. Perhaps you know someone who is still wounded and, on the run, and you've told yourself that it's pointless to fight for their inheritance because they'll never stop running away from God, they'll never surrender and follow the path of the redeeming blood trail that leads to the cross which uses their worse pain to lead them to their greatest calling – salvation in Christ.

> **Perhaps you know someone who is still wounded and, on the run.**

Let me encourage you dear friend, no wounded soul is too far gone for Jesus to rescue because where can I go from your Spirit? Where could I run and hide from your face? If I go up to heaven, you're there! If I go down to the realm of the dead, you're there too! If I fly with wings into the shining dawn, you're there! If I fly into the radiant sunset, you're waiting! Wherever I go, your hand will guide me; your strength will empower me, for your presence is everywhere, bringing light.[6] Each and every wounded soul has a heritage, an inheritance that the hunter, Satan tries to pilfer and plunder. An inheritance is an asset that is passed down after someone dies and you have found the pleasant path that has led you to pleasant places, choosing the Lord as your inheritance because He is our prize, our pleasure, and our portion.[7] And now He calls the bruised and broken ones who have found the redeeming blood trail to become world changers. Like the female elk, we need to work smarter, not harder and develop different strategies depending on the weapon of choice the hunter, Satan decides to use.

A Slightly Ridiculous Woman

Perhaps your children, a family member, or a friend once followed Jesus and now because of wounding they are on the run? Do not worry because there is hope. A woman whom we can learn from is found in the book of second Samuel. Her name is Rizpah. You'd be forgiven if you don't know who she is. Blink and you'll miss her within the story of the war between the house of David and the house of Saul in second Samuel chapter 3. She is only mentioned in one verse, but it is this one power-packed verse that sets the firm foundation of Rizpah becoming a slightly ridiculous woman, whose determination to claim her children's inheritance caught the attention of a king.

They Lost Their Inheritance

I'll set the scene of this family saga that started in 2 Samuel chapter 3 and ends in chapter 21. Abner, King Saul's cousin, decided he was going to sleep with Rizpah, who was a concubine of King Saul. And whether Rizpah wanted to sleep with Abner or not was of no concern to him. However, what Abner did to Rizpah infuriated Ish-Bosheth, Saul's son because he considered it to be high treason against his father, King Saul. 'Abner took advantage of the continuing war between the house of Saul and the house of David to gain power for himself. Saul had a concubine, Rizpah, the daughter of Aiah. One day Ish-Bosheth confronted Abner: 'What business do you have sleeping with my father's concubine?' (2 Samuel 3:6-7) In the ancient world of royal households, a king's concubine was considered to be part of the family. To sleep with one meant that you were suspected of trying to obtain the throne for yourself. Abner was making a statement. Fast forward eighteen more chapters in second Samuel, and we find Rizpah is mentioned again in 2 Samuel chapter 21. Saul is now dead, and David is finally King. However, the land is in famine and David asks God why? The answer that David received from God was that the nation was guilty of not making amends over King Saul's sins. The Gibeonite leaders wanted David to give them seven of Saul's descendants. 'The man who tried to get rid of us, who schemed to wipe us off the map of Israel –well, let seven of his sons be handed over to us to be executed-hanged before God at Gibeah of Saul, the holy mountain.' (2 Samuel 21:5-6) David did as they asked. Unfortunately, two descendants to be hanged were the sons of Rizpah, and on that day the sons didn't just lose their lives, they lost their inheritance.

The sons didn't just lose their lives, they lost their inheritance.

'Rizpah daughter of Aiah took rough burlap and spread it out for herself on a rock from the beginning of the harvest until the heavy rains started. She kept the birds away from the bodies by day and the wild animals by night.' (2 Samuel 21:10) Why would Rizpah do this? Her sons were gone. The war was finished. The house of David had gained victory over the house of Saul, why put herself through this torture? Because Rizpah knew the Torah (the first five books of the Old Testament). She understood the passage in Deuteronomy 21:23, the law which states, '...don't leave the body up there overnight. Bury it that same day because everyone who hangs is cursed by God. Otherwise, you will defile the ground the Eternal your God is giving you to live on.' This slightly ridiculous woman who must have looked like a wild banshee, waving sticks at birds and animals wasn't going to give up. People probably thought she was crazy for acting this way. However, Rizpah wasn't crazy, she was just determined. She was a mother who was not going to let the circumstances that surrounded her two sons dictate their future. They were due their inheritance of a proper royal burial and if it meant Rizpah sat on a hillside next to her dead sons until King David acknowledged that fact, then so be it.

Within my own family, I have watched my children's spiritual inheritance get stolen from them because of someone else's negligence causing them to become wounded and on the run.

> Come back once again and follow the blood trail of Jesus.

The sins of another shaking the very foundation of their faith to the point that their relationship with God died. I, like Rizpah, have sat upon the hillside for many years, praying the wrongs against my children will be made right. Fighting off every vulture and wild animal that the hunter, Satan sends, praying my children will receive their spiritual inheritance and their faith restored, to come back once again and follow the blood trail of Jesus. Why do I do this? Because I need a King to take notice of me. I am going to stand on the promises of the Bible, and I will not move from the hillside until I see my children's spiritual inheritance and salvation restored.

The Inheritance Rizpah was Looking For

King David was told what Rizpah was doing. 'He gathered up their remains and brought them together with the dead bodies of the seven who had just been hanged. The bodies were taken back to the land of Benjamin and given a decent burial in the tomb of Kish, Saul's father.' (2 Samuel 21: 12-14) David knew the Torah passage just as well as Rizpah in Deuteronomy chapter 21, and he acknowledged and honoured her courage and bravery because he didn't want the ground he'd gained to be defiled. For her sons to be buried in the family tomb was the inheritance Rizpah was looking for. Rizpah, a slightly ridiculous woman who inspires and stirs me to continue to spread out upon a rock, clothe myself in rough burlap which is now dirty from fighting off the enemy with sticks, as I continually pray for my children's inheritance and salvation to be restored back to them. I have cried over the corpses of my children's faith,

> **I have cried over the corpses of my children's faith, feeling ridiculous to pray over something that seems so lifeless and still.**

feeling ridiculous to pray over something that seems so lifeless and still. For years I have sat upon that hillside, refusing to give up. Paul encourages the ridiculous ones who wave sticks on hillsides that because we have heard the word of truth – the good news of your salvation – and because you believed in the One who is truth, your lives are marked with His seal. This is none other than the Holy Spirit who was promised as the guarantee toward the inheritance we are to receive when He frees and rescues all who belong to Him. To God be all praise and glory![8]

Like a female elk who feels as though her calves are being threatened, we need to rush to our children's defence, using our hooves and teeth to drive predators and hunters away.

Your Greatest Calling

We need to understand, the process of our restoration can only start when we choose to stop running from our shameful pasts and allow the scars found in Jesus' hands and feet to dry up our blood trail and follow the blood trail Jesus left at the cross. Our submission to God's plan for our lives was never set in stone because in His kindness God always gives us a choice. Joshua 24:15 reminds us that we get to choose this day whom we will serve, as Jesus offers the invitation that frees and rescues all who belong to Him. The moment we stop running is the point of choosing *this day* whom you will serve, and I am always grateful that in all our running, God never leaves us. He's always right behind us just waiting for our resignation to quit running along the *any path* and to find *the path* that leads us to His redemption blood trail. We believe that all our detours and dead ends were never the paths we should have ran down, beating ourselves up because we believe we took a wrong turning. But the revelation I want to share with you is there was only *the* path, the one Jesus follows us on, hoping we would stop running away from Him and run toward him instead. When we allow Him to clean up our wounds so that He can turn our wounds into valuable scars. When we understand that His body was broken and His wine was poured out at the cross happened long before we ever felt the first strike from the hunter, Satan's weapons, it is only then that we can truly know His blood has the power to redeem and restore us.

In the time we've spent together, I hope your healing will help others find their way toward this little wooden cabin in the forest with smoke smouldering out of a metal chimney poking through a grey slatted roof, and the dappled rays of light peeking through the branches of the trees, as they shine their warmth on each petal of the colourful flowers adorning the window boxes neatly positioned either side of the narrow front door. I hope and pray other wounded ones will decide to stop running, take off their muddied shoes and make their selves at home as they pass under the sign above the door frame, that simply says, 'Welcome' finding the same cosy chair you settled yourself in to rest their weary, wounded souls too. Let them know there is a place I've created, a safe place for them to sit awhile, where there is no judgement or fault-finding, just a comforting glow from a log fire that offers them its warmth. A shelter that has been tenderly crafted for those who are tired from the chase of the blood trail. The elks who, when settled in the cosy chair near the fire and are listening to my story as Jesus cleans their wounds with His nail-scarred hands, will look over in the corner of the cabin and find an old desk, it's surface gently marked and graced with the imprints of many prayers written out by hand and given over to our Lord. Heartfelt prayers by the wounded ones who needed a healing touch from the One who was wounded first.

> **It is only then that we can truly know His blood has the power to redeem and restore us.**

Now dear one, as you make your way back out into the forest, you are not who you were when you first found this place. Your wounds have been cleaned, you're now equipped and empowered to stand your ground against the

> You were born for so much more than being wounded and on the run.

hunter, Satan's schemes. Be courageous and bravely take up the powerful armour Jesus left at the cross for you to wear because there is no more running for you. You were born for so much more than being wounded and on the run. So, dear friend, get ready and 'Prepare yourself for the Lord's coming and level a straight path inside your hearts for Him.'⁹ It is time for the overcomers to rise up and use their worst pain to lead others to their greatest calling - SALVATION!

PRAYER

Dear Jesus,
Thank you for leading me to this cabin in the forest so my wounds could be healed. Thank you for showing me Your truths through the life of the elk. Thank you for teaching me how to use each piece of Your armour so I will be able to stand against the hunter, Satan's schemes. Now I am ready to step into my greatest calling; salvation, deliverance, liberation, restoration, and redemption. I don't want to run anymore because You have turned my wounds into valuable scars. Thank you that You sacrificed Yourself on the cross for me. Thank you for Your willingness to be wounded first so I could be healed from my wounds. Now I can use my greatest pain to help other prodigals find the path that flows with

Your redeeming blood trail. The path that leads others who are wounded and, on the run, back to You. Amen.

Endnotes: Chapter Twenty-One

Ref 1 (Quote) Voskamp, Ann. 2016. *The Broken Way: A Daring Path to the Abundant Life.* Grand Rapids, Michigan: Zondervan.

Ref 2 As Female Elk Age, They Learn to Invade Hunters. By Steph Yin, June 15, 2017. https://www.nytimes.com/2017/06/15/science/female-elk-hunters.html

Ref 3 Female elk are practically bulletproof by age 9. By Sarah Fecht June 17, 2017.

Ref 4 Luke 10:34 Syswerda, Jean, and Faith Organization. 2001. *NIV Women of Faith Study Bible: New International Version.* Grand Rapids, Mich.: Zondervan.

Ref 5 Romans 8:35-37 Syswerda, Jean, and Faith Organization. 2001. *NIV Women of Faith Study Bible: New International Version.* Grand Rapids, Mich.: Zondervan.

Ref 6 Psalm 139:7-11 *The Passion Translation: New Testament with Psalms, Proverbs, and Song of Songs, Second Edition.* Passion & Fire Ministries, Inc. BroadStreet Publishing: 2018.

Ref 7 Psalm 16:5-6 *The Passion Translation: New Testament with Psalms, Proverbs, and Song of Songs, Second Edition.* Passion & Fire Ministries, Inc. BroadStreet Publishing: 2018.

Story of Rizpah. All passages. Peterson, Eugene H. 2000. *The Message Bible:* Colorado Springs, Colorado. Navpress.

Ref 8 Ephesians 1:13-14 Ecclesia Bible Society. 2012. *The Voice Bible: Step into the Story of Scripture.* Nashville: Thomas Nelson.

Ref 9 Matthew 3:3 *The Passion Translation: New Testament with Psalms, Proverbs, and Song of Songs, Second Edition.* Passion & Fire Ministries, Inc. BroadStreet Publishing: 2018.

I Will Get Up and Go to My Father

Dear friend,

I don't want to leave you just yet because I wouldn't let you to go back out into the forest without giving you an opportunity of knowing Jesus personally. In chapter eleven, I talked about the recovery of the elk and share the parable of the prodigal son. Found in Luke chapter 15, the lost son had to come to his senses before he was ready to find his identity.

'But when he [finally] came to his senses, he said, 'How many of my father's hired men have more than enough food, while I am dying here of hunger! I will get up and go to my father, and I'll say to him, 'Father, I have sinned against heaven and in your sight. I am no longer worthy to be called your son; [just] treat me like one of your hired men." (Luke 15:17-19 Amp Bible)

The Father doesn't want to treat you like one of His hired servants, He wants you to become His son or His daughter. 'Quickly bring out the best robe [for the guest of honor] and put it on him; and give him a ring for his hand, and sandals for his feet...for this son of mine was [as good as] dead and is alive again; he was lost and has been found.' (Luke 15:22-24 Amp Bible)

What about you dear friend? Are you ready to come to your senses and allow the Father to clothe you in your inheritance? As I have mentioned before, the Father stands by the gate and waits for you dear son or daughter to come home.

Salvation Prayer

Jesus,
I'm sorry I ran away from You. Forgive me of all my sins and come into my heart. I believe You died on the cross for me, and rose again so I could find redemption. From this moment on, I trust You and I will follow You all the days of my life. Amen.

One More Thing Before You Go

If you've just prayed that prayer out loud, I encourage you to find a local Christian church so you can continue your journey of discipleship.

ACKNOWLEDGEMENTS

The book you hold in your hands could not have been possible without the help and encouragement of some everyday heroes. These are the ones who not only believed in the message this book carried but understood that no one should be ashamed of showing people their scars.

The Wollongong Sisterhood. When the journey of becoming a published author seemed too hard, too difficult, or too impossible, you became my cheer squad. We've laughed together and cried together along the path. Thank you for being a constant reminder to never settle for less than God's best. I truly love each one of you. Now, raise your coffee cup to more shenanigans!

Leonie Schlosser. My dearest friend. You've known my journey of wounding long before I was able to find the words to write them down on paper. From my heart to yours, thank you for reminding me that, "I am enough."

Karyn Rusin. Whenever we meet, one of us ends up crying! Thank you for your friendship and for believing in me. I wouldn't have made it this far without your encouragement.

Ivana McNeil. Dear friend. Thank you for always cheering me on in my writing.

Nicole Partridge. Thank you for looking me square in the eye and telling me I'm a writer. The gravity of those words felt like anointing oil poured onto me from the Lord. You have believed wholeheartedly in this project from the start.

Elizabeth Chapman. Who'd have thought a simple "Hello" would lead you to becoming my publisher? But more importantly, throughout our journey of 'Wounded' you have become a close friend. You're a dream to work with and you inspire me constantly with your revelations! I am forever grateful for your gifts of vulnerability, love, and support in reaching people with the message of Jesus.

My husband, Philip. We have journeyed together for over thirty-two years and from the moment I met you I knew without a shadow of a doubt you would always have my back. Thank you for your steadfastness and for never allowing my wounds to become excuses to not make a difference in this world. I'll love you forever.

My children, Samuel, and Lauren. I am honoured and humbled to be your mother. Thank you for always encouraging me to go after my dreams and to share my story with courage and boldness. You two are my greatest joy and treasure. And yes, you are both my favourite.

And finally, Jesus. The hero of this story. Your sacrificial, unfailing, unending love has left me free and undone. I thank You over and over again for all those years you waited at the gate, kept Your eyes on the horizon, and welcomed this prodigal home again. Thank you for turning my wounds into valuable scars.

www.ingramcontent.com/pod-product-compliance
Lightning Source LLC
Chambersburg PA
CBHW070251010526
44107CB00056B/2420